Spiritual Boot Camp

BASIC TRAINING FOR
SPIRITUAL WARFARE

Dr. Patricia Venegas

SPIRITUAL BOOT CAMP: Basic Training for Spiritual Warfare
Copyright 2023 by Patricia Venegas

Critical Mass Books
Haymarket, Virginia
www.criticalmasspublishing.com

2nd Edition

ISBN: 978-1-947153-48-6

Cover Design   Thom Meredith Jr.
Interior Layout   Rachel Newhouse

Unless otherwise indicated, Biblical quotes in this book are from New King James Version®. Copyright © 1982 by Thomas Nelson. Used by permission. All rights reserved.

Contents

AUTHOR'S NOTE | i

ACKNOWLEDGMENTS | iii

INTRODUCTION | vii

PRAYER OF PREPARATION | xix

CHAPTER ONE | 1
Your Call and Purpose

CHAPTER TWO | 19
Bind Up the Broken Heart To Set the Captive Free

CHAPTER THREE | 23
Erika's Story

CHAPTER FOUR | 35
Puss Pockets and Trigger Events

CHAPTER FIVE | 43
Emotional Healing

CHAPTER SIX | 49
Accepted, and Loved In the Beloved

CHAPTER SEVEN | 55
You Have Been Forgiven

CHAPTER EIGHT | 63
Repentance

CHAPTER NINE | 71
Unforgiveness

CHAPTER TEN | 81
Generational Curses

CHAPTER ELEVEN | 89
Word Curses and Cursed Objects

CHAPTER TWELVE | 97
Soul Ties and Inner Vows

CHAPTER THIRTEEN | 105
The Spirit of Intimidation and Jezebel

CHAPTER FOURTEEN | 117
Paganism

CHAPTER FIFTEEN | 121
Pagan Deities that Come Beside Us

CHAPTER SIXTEEN | 125
It Is in the Foundation

CHAPTER SEVENTEEN | 129
God's Feasts

CHAPTER EIGHTEEN | 135
Harlotry

CHAPTER NINETEEN | 143
Some Spirits Which Cause Pain and Suffering

CHAPTER TWENTY | 147
Drugs and Alcohol

CHAPTER TWENTY-ONE | 153
Canceling Satan's Special Assignments and Attacks

CHAPTER TWENTY-TWO | 159
Prayer and Fasting

CLOSING THOUGHTS | 167

Author's Note

Having been raised as a traditional Christian with denominational values, my desperate need for spiritual understanding in my ministry led me to ask God for answers to questions I didn't know how to ask.

I then began studying the Bible from a Hebrew perspective. During my studies, I learned the Hebrew names for God, Lord, Jesus, and the Holy Spirit.

- God is Elohim
- The LORD is Yehovah
- Jesus is Yeshua
- The Holy Spirit is Ruach Hakodesh

LORD (YHVH): The Tetragrammaton from Greek: τετραγράμματον, meaning "consisting of four letters." In the Hebrew bible, God reveals His name to Israel as Yehovah over 6,700 times. When vowels are added to YHVH, the name reads Yehovah.

God (Elohim): "Elohim" denotes what linguists call a "plural of majesty, honor, or fullness." That is, he is GOD in the total sense of the word. He is "GOD of gods" or literally, "Elohei of HaElohim" (See: Deuteronomy 10:17 & Psalm 136:2).

The Holy Spirit (Ruach Hakodesh): is sent by Yehovah and is His most crucial and precious part. He has given Him to those of us who believe in Yeshua. *"However, when He, the Spirit of truth, has come, He will guide you into all truth; for He will not speak on His own authority, but whatever He hears He will speak; and He will tell you things to come."* (John 16:13)

In this book, I will refer to Jesus by His Hebrew name, Yeshua. It means "Yehovah, (the LORD Yehovah), is Salvation." Salvation denotes a complete restoration according to Strong's Hebrew Concordance #3468. It means salvation, deliverance, rescue, safety, and welfare.

Salvation is all-inclusive: spiritual, emotional, moral, social, relational, and ultimately life eternal, by the power of the blood of Yeshua at Calvary. Yeshua's blood has bought and paid for our salvation. Still, the continued work of becoming God's (Elohim's) holy people is a life-long journey of presenting ourselves to God (Elohim) and the Holy Spirit (Ruach Hakodesh) for transformation.

Our loving and gracious God (Elohim) desires us to be whole in all aspects.

Acknowledgments

First and foremost, I would like to praise and thank God, the Almighty, who has granted countless blessings and sent my Lord and Savior, Yeshua, for my healing, deliverance, and restoration. I would hate to think where I would be today if it had not been for Him.

I want to thank my husband, Reverend Benjamin, especially. You are the wind beneath my wings, allowing me to grow and be all God has called me to be. Without your love and support, none of this would be possible. Thank you so much; I love you with all of my heart.

I also want to thank my children, Pamela, Deborah, Thomas, Michelle, Kelly, and Stephanie, my grandchildren, and great-grandchildren. I am forever grateful to the Lord for allowing me to be your mother, grandmother, and great-grandmother. You all are such amazing people.

I take this opportunity to express my gratitude to the people who have been instrumental in completing this book. Thank you, Pastor Reina Wendel, Pastor Mary Fernandez, Pastor Abigail Scoggins, Maria (Toni), Mario Luna, and my son Thom Meredith for all the hours you have sacrificed. You have added so much to it. Thank you for your wisdom, knowledge, and support.

Thank you to everyone who contributed to this book through your testimony. *"And they overcame him by the blood of the Lamb, and by the word of their testimony; and they loved not their lives unto the death."* (Revelation 12:11)

Ask Yourself...

_____ Do you sometimes wonder why the same recurring and trying events keep happening to you?

_____ Have you ever felt like you're rejected or abandoned?

_____ Do you sometimes feel emotional pain and anguish?

_____Do you feel like you are spiritually battling within your soul?

_____ Is there a desire within your heart to be free from evil feelings or thoughts?

_____ Would you like to live a victorious life?

_____Would you like to go to another level spiritually, in your Christian walk?

If you answered "Yes," to any of these questions, this book was written for you.

Introduction

MY VISION

The Lord gave me a vision of a rich man in the nineteenth century. He was traveling down a cobblestone street in a buggy drawn by a horse. Off to his right-hand side was a group of enslaved people. They were chained to a metal stake and forced to crouch down. Their clothes were ripped and threadbare, and it was apparent they had been beaten, starved, and abused. The rich man had incredible compassion for them, so he went to their master, a wicked man, and said, "How much for all those slaves?"

Although the wicked man thought, "They're worthless," he named a high price.

The rich man had compassion and bought the slaves and set them free. At first, they were very excited. They went into the streets and celebrated. But they did not know what to do when night fell because they had never experienced freedom. So, they returned, sat down, and put the chains back on because they had only known bondage.

The Lord revealed to me that Yeshua is that rich man, Satan is the wicked man, and we're the chained and abused slaves. When we first get saved, we are so excited. However, we've never walked this way, we don't know how to be free, and many of us return to familiar chains and fetters.

> *"As a dog returns to his own vomit, so a fool repeats his folly." (Proverbs 26:11)*

I pray that you will use the weapons you will learn from this book to walk in the freedom God has provided for you.

THE WAR WE FIGHT

You may not realize it, but you are in a great spiritual war. It's the war of the ages, which has caused every other war in the history of humanity. It is the war between good and evil, God and Satan, and you are right in the middle. Make no mistake, and you are part of this war.

PREPARE FOR THE SPIRITUAL FIGHT!

Spiritual Boot Camp Basic Training for Warfare will teach you how to live an empowered life as a firm believer endowed with the authority, power, and confidence you can only get from the truth of Elohim's Word. It will prepare you for spiritual warfare and VICTORY!

TWO SPIRITUAL KINGDOMS AT WAR

Two spiritual kingdoms are at war—the heavenly kingdom under God's rule and an earthly (worldly) kingdom under Satan's rule.

This war started in heaven with an angel named Lucifer. He was a beautifully angel created by God and was part of the kingdom of God. He rebelled against God because he wanted to be like the Most High and was expelled from heaven by Elohim.

> *"How you are fallen from Heaven, O Lucifer, son of the morning! How you are cut down to the ground, you who weakened the nations! For you have said in your heart: 'I will ascend into Heaven; I will exalt my throne above the stars of God. I will also sit on the mount of the congregation on the farthest sides of the north. I will ascend above the heights of the clouds; I will be like the Most High.' Yet you shall be brought down to Sheol, To the lowest depths of the Pit." (Isaiah 14:12-15)*

A group of angels joined Lucifer (a.k.a. Satan) in this rebellion, and there was war in Heaven.

The invisible war against man began in the Garden of Eden. Satan caused Adam and Eve to sin, resulting in all people inheriting a sinful nature and committing individual acts of sin. *"Wherefore, as by one man sin entered into the world, and death by sin; and so, death passed upon all men, for all have sinned."* (Romans 5:12)

The following scriptures refer to the war against Israel and the followers of Yeshua because we are grafted into Israel.

> *"And the dragon was enraged with the woman, and he went to make war with the rest of her offspring, who keep the commandments of God and have the testimony of Jesus Christ." (Revelation 12:17)*

> *"For if the first fruit is holy, the lump is also holy; and if the root is holy, so are the branches. And if some of the branches were broken off, and you, being a wild olive tree, were grafted in among them, and with them became a partaker of the root and fatness of the olive tree, do not boast against the branches. But if you do boast, remember that you do not support the root, but the root supports you." (Romans 11:16-18)*

SATAN HAS LEGAL RIGHTS

In Ephesians chapter six, Paul tells us that our battle is not against flesh and blood but with the powers of darkness. *"Finally, my brethren, be strong in the Lord and the power of His might. Put on the whole armor of God that you may be able to stand against the wiles of the devil, for we do not wrestle against flesh and blood, but against principalities, against powers, against the rulers of the darkness of this age, against spiritual hosts of wickedness in the heavenly places. Therefore, take up the whole armor of God, that you may be able to withstand in the evil day, and having done all, to stand."* (Ephesians 6:10-13)

In this book, you will learn about Satan's legal rights, how to remove those rights, win your battles, and be strong in the Lord and the power of His might.

THIS WAR IS FOR YOUR VERY SOUL

Have you ever heard of someone selling their soul to the devil? Satan strives for your soul. This war is for your soul, and the battle is between God and Satan. Your final destination is either heaven or hell.

YOU ARE SOUL, SPIRIT, AND FLESH

You are a soul with a spirit that lives within your flesh, and your fleshly body is the vessel that houses your soul.

Your soul has three parts—your mind, emotions, and will. In Psalm 23:3, David says, *"He restores my soul and leads me in paths of righteousness for His name's sake."*

YOUR MIND IS THE BATTLEFIELD

One of the most critical things in this battle is learning to guard, strengthen, and renew your mind.

> *"For though we walk in the flesh, we do not war according to the flesh. For the weapons of our warfare are not carnal but mighty in God for pulling down strongholds, casting down arguments and every high thing that exalts itself against the knowledge of God, bringing every thought into captivity to the obedience of Christ, and being ready to punish all disobedience when your obedience is fulfilled." (2 Corinthians 10:3-5)*

You must renew your mind with the Word of God to win the battle. We use our swords as part of our armor in this fight. *"The sword of the Spirit, which is the word of God."* (Ephesians 6:17b)

Yeshua used the scriptures to win His battle with Satan in the wilderness.

> *"Then Jesus, being filled with the Holy Spirit, returned from the Jordan, and was led by the Spirit into the wilderness, being tempted for forty days by the devil. And in those days, He ate nothing, and afterward, when they had ended, He was hungry. And the devil said to Him, "If You are the Son of*

God, command this stone to become bread." But Jesus answered him, saying, "It is written, 'Man shall not live by bread alone, but by every word of God.'" Then the devil, taking Him up on a high mountain, showed Him all the kingdoms of the world in a moment of time. And the devil said to Him, "All this authority I will give You, and their glory; for this has been delivered to me, and I give it to whomever I wish. Therefore, if You will worship before me, all will be Yours." And Jesus answered and said to him, "Get behind Me, Satan! For it is written, 'You shall worship the Lord your God, and Him only you shall serve.'" Then he brought Him to Jerusalem, set Him on the pinnacle of the temple, and said to Him, "If You are the Son of God, throw Yourself down from here. For it is written: 'He shall give His angels charge over you, to keep you,' and, 'In their hands they shall bear you up, lest you dash your foot against a stone.'" And Jesus answered and said to him, "It has been said, 'You shall not tempt the Lord your God.'" Now when the devil had ended every temptation, he departed from Him until an opportune time." (Luke 4:1-13)

YOUR EMOTIONS NEED TO BE HEALED

Satan uses the pains of your heart to put you in a prison house emotionally. You need to have your emotions healed to win this battle. Yeshua was sent to bind up the broken hearts and free the captives.

"The Spirit of the Lord God is upon Me Because the Lord has anointed Me to preach good tidings to the

poor; He has sent Me to heal the brokenhearted, to proclaim liberty to the captives, And the opening of the prison to those who are bound." (Isaiah 61:1)

"So, He came to Nazareth, where He had been brought up. And as His custom was, He went into the synagogue on the Sabbath day and stood up to read. And He was handed the book of the prophet Isaiah. And when He had opened the book, He found the place where it was written:

"The Spirit of the Lord is upon Me Because He has anointed Me To preach the gospel to the poor; He has sent Me to heal the brokenhearted, to proclaim liberty to the captives and recovery of sight to the blind, to set at liberty those who are oppressed. To proclaim the acceptable year of the Lord." (Luke 4:16-19)

YOUR WILL NEEDS TO LINE UP WITH THE WILL OF GOD

You have been brought into His Kingdom and must submit your will to His. *"Not everyone who says to Me, 'Lord, Lord,' shall enter the Kingdom of heaven, but he who does the will of My Father in heaven."* (Matthew 7:21)

YOUR FLESH MUST BE CRUCIFIED

The desire of your flesh resists your transformation into becoming all the Lord has for you, and Satan wants to use the pleasures of your flesh to keep you enslaved to your old habits and sinful attitudes. Denying sin requires daily choices. You crucify your flesh when you choose God's way instead of sin.

Satan is called the prince of the air and wants you to disobey your heavenly Father.

> *"And you He made alive, who were dead in trespasses and sins, in which you once walked according to the course of this world, according to the prince of the power of the air, the spirit who now works in the sons of disobedience, among whom also we all once conducted ourselves in the lusts of our flesh, fulfilling the desires of the flesh and of the mind, and were by nature children of wrath, just as the others." (Ephesians 2:1-3)*

> *"I say then: Walk in the Spirit, and you shall not fulfill the lust of the flesh. For the flesh lusts against the Spirit, and the Spirit against the flesh; and these are contrary to one another, so that you do not do the things that you wish. But if you are led by the Spirit, you are not under the law. Now the works of the flesh are evident, which are: adultery, fornication, uncleanness, lewdness, idolatry, sorcery, hatred, contentions, jealousies, outbursts of wrath, selfish ambitions, dissensions, heresies, envy, murders, drunkenness, revelries, and the like; of which I tell you beforehand, just as I also told you in*

> *time past, that those who practice such things will not inherit the Kingdom of God." (Galatians 5:16-21)*

> *"Those who are Christ's have crucified the flesh with its passions and desires." (Galatians 5:24)*

YOUR SPIRIT MUST BE BORN AGAIN

Your Spirit becomes born again (regenerated by the Holy Spirit) when you ask Yeshua to come into your heart and give your life to the Lord.

> *"Jesus answered and said to him, "Most assuredly, I say to you, unless one is born again, he cannot see the kingdom of God." Nicodemus said to Him, "How can a man be born when he is old? Can he enter a second time into his mother's womb and be born?" Jesus answered, "Most assuredly, I say to you, unless one is born of water and the Spirit, he cannot enter the Kingdom of God. That which is born of the flesh is flesh, and that which is born of the Spirit is Spirit." (John 3:3-6)*

YESHUA CAME TO PREACH THE KINGDOM OF GOD

The kingdom's message encompasses restoration, physical and emotional healing, and deliverance.

> *"When the sun was setting, all those who had any that were sick with various diseases*

brought them to Him; and He laid His hands on every one of them and healed them. And demons also came out of many, crying out and saying, "You are the Christ, the Son of God!" And He, rebuking them, did not allow them to speak, for they knew that He was the Christ. Now, when it was day, He departed and went into a deserted place. And the crowd sought Him and came to Him and tried to keep Him from leaving them; but He said to them, **"I must preach the kingdom of God to the other cities also because for this purpose I have been sent."** *(Luke 4:40-43)*

"And these signs will follow those who believe: In My name they will cast out demons; they will speak with new tongues; they will take up serpents; and if they drink anything deadly, it will by no means hurt them; they will lay hands on the sick, and they will recover." (Mark 16:17-20)

Prayer Of Preparation

Before reading this book, pray this Prayer of Preparation.

Prayer: Father, I come before You into the throne room of grace. I call my mind into submission to You. Let Your thoughts be my thoughts, and Your ways be my ways. Let me not be distracted or hindered in any way. Your Word says, *"'You shall love the Lord your God with all your heart, soul, and mind;' This is the first and great commandment. And the second is like it: 'You shall love your neighbor as yourself.'"* Give me the grace to love you with all of my heart, soul, and mind and to love others as myself. Circumcise my heart, remove my stony heart, and give me a heart of flesh. Write Your precepts on it so that I can serve You wholeheartedly. Remove the walls that Satan has built around my heart to keep me from feeling loved and loving others.

Your Word says: "Who is blind but Your servant who has eyes but does not see." Remove the scales and blinders from my eyes. Allow me to see the enemy's schemes as if I were wearing night goggles. Give me Your spiritual eyes of understanding.

Your Word says: "Who is deaf but my servant who has ears but can't hear." Lord, unplug my ears so that I may hear Your commanding voice, as if I had a walkie-talkie that is turned up to total volume.

Purify my lips so that my words would be seasoned with salt and bring grace to others. James 3:6 states, *"The tongue is a fire, a world of iniquity."* James 3:9 states, *"With our tongue we bless our God and Father, and with it, we curse men, who have been made in the likeness of God."* Please touch my mouth and put Your Words in my mouth.

Your Word says in Hosea 4:6, *"My people are destroyed for lack of knowledge."* I repent for rejecting knowledge. Please give me knowledge, understanding, and wisdom. I want to bear much fruit for Your glory. In Yeshua's name, I pray. Amen.

THE SCRIPTURES REFERENCED IN THE "PRAYER OF PREPARATION."

"Teacher, which is the great commandment in the law?" Jesus said to him, "'You shall love the Lord your God with all your heart, with all your soul, and with all your mind.' This is the first and great commandment.

And the second is like it: 'You shall love your neighbor as yourself.' On these two commandments hang all the Law and the Prophets." (Matthew 22:36-40)

"Hear this now, O foolish people, without understanding, who have eyes and see not, and who have ears and hear not."—Jeremiah 5:21

"Hear you deaf; and look, you blind, that you may see. Who is blind but My servant, or deaf as My messenger whom I send? Who is blind as he who is perfect, and blind as the Lord's servant? Seeing many things, but you do not observe; opening the ears, but he does not hear." (Isaiah 42:18-20)

"That the God of our Lord Jesus, the Father of glory, may give to you the spirit of wisdom and revelation in the knowledge of Him, the eyes of your understanding being enlightened; that you may know what is the hope of His calling, what are the riches of the glory of His inheritance in the saints, and what is the exceeding greatness of His power toward us who believe, according to the working of His mighty power." (Ephesians 1:17-19)

"I will give you a new heart and put a new spirit within you; I will take the heart of stone out of your flesh and give you a heart of flesh." (Ezekiel 36:26)

"My people are destroyed for lack of knowledge. Because you have rejected knowledge, I also will reject you from being priest for Me; because you have forgotten the law of your Elohim, I also will forget your children." (Hosea 4:6)

CHAPTER ONE

Your Call and Purpose

You have been called into the kingdom of God for such a time as this, and the Lord has a call and purpose for you. When we come into our Christian walk, many of us bring in traditions that have been passed down to us through generations. We don't question why we follow these traditions. They are not scriptural and hinder our call and purpose.

> *"Train up a child in the way he should go, and when he is old, he will not depart from it." (Proverbs 22:6)*

Yeshua told the Pharisees their traditions made the Word of God to no effect. *"Making the Word of God of no effect through your tradition which you have handed down. And many such things you do."* (Mark 7:13)

Elizabeth's story is an excellent example of how we can bring our traditions into our walk with God. Satan tried to kill her, the Word tells us, *"My people are destroyed for lack of knowledge."* (Hosea 4:6). She is now ministering in a very powerful way to the Hispanic community in the United States and Mexico.

ELIZABETH'S STORY

As a young child, I loved God. I would consistently walk to the local church, sit and talk with God for hours, and wait with hope to hear back from Him. I saw people come to worship for miracles, and healings. I thought that if I lit ten more candles and bowed down for hours over the saint's feet, he would answer me.

Other times, desperation took me there. I'd sit in a back pew in silence, asking God, "Do you exist, are you hearing me?"

My grandmother was very dedicated to the things of God and had great faith. I have memories of visiting her in Mexico and her taking me to the local cathedrals where people would come in on their knees and bow low to the altar. Some lit candles to the saints, and others anointed themselves with holy water. As a young girl, I thought this was the usual practice of faith.

My life was not always easy. I was dedicated to the occult at a very young age. It was in my family lineage, and seeing things in the occult was not out of the norm.

To give you a little background, I grew up in a home where my parents didn't always have the best relationship. There was a lot of division and dysfunction. My father wouldn't always come home; when he did, he would often be drunk. I would awaken to them screaming and hitting each other. My heart was in perpetual panic. I would, at times, face the wall in my room and cover my head with a sheet in hopes that it would all go away.

My mother would lose sleep waiting for my father to come home. I would hear her crying with loud, desperate sobs in her room, not knowing where he was. She would drive the streets looking for him late at night. Besides the many nights of losing sleep, I had my demons to fight—I was being consistently sexually abused. How could I ever tell my mom and dad when they had their problems?

The abuse continued for a few years until I finally decided to speak out. I was on the top bunk bed, and I had awakened to prepare for how I would end my nightmare. I told myself that when he came into the room and began to touch my body, I would scream so loud everyone in the house would hear me. Then they would know the truth. Well, it didn't quite go that way. He came in as usual and began to try to touch me. He reeked of alcohol. I remember trying to scream but was paralyzed with fear and couldn't make a sound. Something fell. I knew it was God because nothing could've made that noise. It spooked him, and he ran out of my room.

I remember shaking and running to my parent's room and telling them I had been abused for a long time and couldn't take it anymore. The following day, I woke up to a phone conversation my mom was having. She was speaking to the man abusing me, and he defended himself and told her I was lying. I immediately felt unprotected, betrayed, unloved, unworthy, and angry. I made a vow never again to tell anyone anything that was happening to me or to trust anyone. No one ever asked me anything about the abuse or if I needed help, and it was taboo in my home to talk about anything that was happening or my emotions.

Two weeks later, my mother took me to a "therapist." We drove up to a gorgeous home on a hillside. We entered through the back door and walked into a small waiting area. A beautiful woman approached us as I sat there and I wondered what I was doing there. She asked me to come into her private room. As I sat there, I looked around. I saw an altar of saints, and amid the saints were beautiful dolls made of wood carvings. The dolls were dressed in beautiful garments with expensive jewelry. There were candles and fresh flowers. She pulled out a stack of tarot cards and began to shuffle them. As she pulled the cards from the pile, she turned them over and looked at them. Then she looked at me without saying a word. I had never experienced anything like that. She asked me questions about myself that had nothing to do with my sexual abuse. She asked me if I was okay with her being my friend. I said yes. Later she would become my "godmother." In this occult practice, it is common to have a godmother or a godfather upon initiation to the "religion."

She invited me to spend time with her in her home. I agreed. As time went by, we began to build a close relationship. She treated me like I was her daughter. I even had a room in her house. She had a massive pool, which drew me back because I love to swim. She had a small shack behind her home. We were not allowed to enter or even go near it. For years I had no idea what was in there; so I dismissed it. When I would spend the night, she came to my room at midnight and asked me to join her. We would walk downstairs and go into her garage. She had prepared a washing—what we call a limpia. There was a pentagram on the floor in the center of the garage, and she created it with white chalk. In the middle of the pentagram was a basin big enough to baptize a person. It was full of warm water with the scent of flowers and perfume. Many plants were prepared and pre-cooked, and whole eggs were in a bowl. There were candles, "holy water," and clean white clothes to wear after the ceremony; this was not uncommon, for I have seen this my whole life.

In the Mexican roots, traditional medicine and healers have been around for centuries. They are called Curanderos (healers), who are supposed to guide you with good luck, love, finances, and balance. The truth is, Curanderos (healers) are witches and warlocks.

Limpia is a spiritual cleansing; they believe balance is restored through it, and because I was abused, I was a perfect candidate for this ceremony. It's a cleansing ritual where the healer uses herbs, cold water or mezcal (alcohol), a chicken egg, fire, or copal smoke (believed to purify the energy of spaces), to bring you back into balance. Vision guides are used through the spirits to seek guidance. Others read your iris, which is "the third eye." Still, others diagnose you with the chicken egg. They may feel your pulse or read the fire, smoke, earth, and water—all the earth's elements. They work with ceremonies, rituals, candles, healing with sacred plants, or through massages. Much of what we call the New Age today is rooted in this.

Shortly before I gave my life to Jesus, I had many problems due to years of getting therapy from my godmother and being involved with Santeria. Each visit cost $1,500, which affected my financial resources. There were times when the price was even higher as I sought more power and healing. At first, I would see quick results. But they were only temporary, and it wasn't long before the situation worsened.

I got to a place where I felt I would lose my mind—not to mention that I had demonic visitations. The demonic activity would increase at night, moving in and out of my bedroom while I tried to sleep. I could hear the diabolical conversations as they whispered. I listened to their voices accusing me. A strong spirit of suicide wanted me to end my life. When I was 16, I took a whole bottle of sleeping pills and ended up in the ICU. I constantly thought of killing myself and how to leave this earth. Maybe I could drive my car into a pole or off a bridge. I felt like I was going insane. There was nothing but doom and gloom. I was in utter depression and desperate for help. My first marriage was falling apart. I was reliving my mom's life, and I didn't understand ancestral sins. I now know this was a generational curse on me.

THE LITTLE SHACK IN THE BACK

About the little shack in the back of the house—My godmother told me she would help by placing me at the center of the highest form of healing where I could ask for anything. I was oblivious to what this meant, and desperate measures sometimes led me to make ignorant decisions. I didn't know I would become a sacrifice to Satan. But I agreed to do this if this would fix my many problems.

When I entered the shack, there was a cauldron. The cauldron, (a large metal pot), is a symbol of witchcraft related to evil spells invoked to bring death and control the elements of the earth. I looked around, and at my feet were bones of dead animal remains. Blood was splattered on the walls, and the smell of death surrounded me.

As my godmother walked out the door, leaving me in the cauldron, she told me I could ask for anything. All I wanted was for my marriage to be healed and to be healed emotionally. I was seeking peace because I didn't want to be depressed, anxious, afraid, jealous, unloved, or worthless anymore.

I was neutralized by what I saw in that shack. I thought it was normal and felt like I could ask for anything. I closed my eyes and held my nose to the smell.

Shortly after leaving that day, I almost got into a car accident. The intense feeling of wanting to die went from 10 to 100. I even wrote a suicide letter to my family. I was going to end the torment. I thought not even God would help me.

A week later, my sister invited me to a healing encounter. I was angry with her because she kept insisting, I go. I figured since I was going to kill myself, I'd do this one good deed for her so she would remember how much I loved her.

I am amazed at how the Lord hears our cries and tries to get us to the place to be healed and delivered; this was a game-changer for me. I encountered the presence of the Lord—it was so strong. The pastor began to talk about the occult and the new age movement and all affiliated with it, as well as how Satan operates through those things. I had been raised to believe nothing was wrong with white magic, and I thought it to be true because I lacked understanding. There was an altar call, and I accepted Jesus as my Lord and Savior. The pastor asked us to close our eyes for prayer. He then had us pray after him to renounce the occult practices. The stronger the prayer got, the more I began to feel angry and anxious. The Lord showed me visions of everything in which I was involved. As I saw the images, the tormentors came to demand my soul. I could feel their stronghold on me. I was their property. I saw demons running around and tormenting the people. I heard the cries of these people as they were being delivered and set free. I couldn't believe what I was seeing.

I saw demons waiting for me, and I knew they were death and hades. As they began to pull me in, I screamed and cried for help and could feel the torment. This was a fight for my soul. Suddenly death began to wrap itself around my throat like a massive python.

At first, the demons refused to leave me because they had legal rights to my soul, not only because of the occult doors I had opened but also because I was holding people in unforgiveness. I remember hearing a woman praying over me, and it seemed like a circle of fire was around me. The harder she prayed, the more that demonic spirit of death choked me.

The woman praying for me wanted me to say Jesus, but something held my tongue. I tried many times but couldn't say His name. It felt like a horrible nightmare I couldn't escape. The deliverance lasted five hours. I was exhausted, and I had no fight left in me.

A woman came to me, and I heard her say, "Say in the name of Jesus now." At that point, I said His name and an enormous scream came out of me. It was as if I had come out of the ICU and felt I could breathe again. I could see. The fog lifted. I couldn't stop weeping. The Lord was so good to me. It was at that moment I knew the power His name possessed.

I had been in so much warfare, tormented by the demonic realm. I couldn't believe what I had been involved with and couldn't understand how the woman called my "godmother"— who professed love for me— could be so evil. I had been so blinded.

The following day I received the Baptism of the Holy Spirit. I thought I was completely free and done. It was over, and I wouldn't ever have to experience anything like that again. When I accepted the Lord, I didn't know that being healed and delivered was a process. I didn't understand the severity of the legal rights I had given to the demonic realm or the hurts and pains I had buried. I still had battles to fight. My journey lasted 12 more years.

After my salvation, I had some severe issues, and I didn't realize I still needed emotional healing. That part got skipped over. Demons showed up at night while I would try to sleep, and I wanted to pretend it was not happening again after those long hours of deliverance and prayer. I was fearful and anxious and didn't understand how I could be saved and still experience spiritual battles.

I would ask our senior leadership for prayer, which would not help. They would misjudge, dismiss, or accuse me of opening doors to give the enemy the legal right to torment me. They thought I must be in sin, or some thought I wasn't even saved. I felt like I was an unworthy and unloved project by some people. I thought I needed to pray more, and maybe I didn't love God enough that I missed it, or was unaware of my shortcomings. I worked hard to improve myself and to be loved. It was exhausting and shameful.

After eleven years of suffering, my church offered a program for healing. At first, I remember being hesitant about starting anything like this. I struggled with being vulnerable, opening my heart to people, and letting them know my real issues. I had seen enough in the church to honestly never ask for help, not to mention the severe problems from past church hurts and disappointment.

But my desire for healing was so intense that I decided to surrender to the Holy Spirit and let him submerge me fully. I love God, and I was ready to fight for my freedom. I always felt there was more to my walk with the Lord than this wilderness, and I wanted to be healed emotionally.

The healing program started well, but about halfway through, I felt vulnerable. The emotions, pain, and feelings were surreal. It felt like I was having open heart surgery; my past childhood wounds were entirely front and center. I couldn't push the memories down any longer, and everything was so intense. I was so terrified of the dark at night that I had to keep all the lights and the television on.

I didn't understand how I could relive this. I was taught Christians could not have demons. Someone told me that if anyone is in Christ, he is a new creation; old things have passed away, and all things have become new. So, I didn't have to look back at my past—only go forward.

The Lord was taking me into a season of true healing. He kept giving me Isaiah 61:1-3 in the Bible.

> *"The Spirit of the Lord God is upon Me, because the Lord has anointed Me to preach good tidings to the poor; He has sent Me to heal the brokenhearted, to proclaim liberty to the captives, and the opening of the prison to those who are bound; to proclaim the acceptable year of the Lord, and the day of vengeance of our God; to comfort all who mourn, to console those who mourn in Zion, to give them beauty for ashes, the oil of joy for mourning, the garment of praise for the spirit of heaviness; That they may be called trees of righteousness, the planting of the Lord, that He may be glorified." (Isaiah 61:1-3)*

During my sleep, He would give me the names of demons—Ashtoreth, Baal, Harlotry, Molech, etc.

To my surprise, as I studied the Bible, I would find the names that the Lord had given me. But I still did not understand what the Lord was doing.

Nothing made sense, and I remember waking up one morning feeling like this was it. I was in a sick bed near death, and it felt like my heart would stop beating. The feelings were so intense that I debated about driving to the ER.

A family member told me about a ministry that helped her: *Without Spot or Wrinkle Ministries International*, which includes inner healing and deliverance.

When I walked into *Without Spot or Wrinkle Ministries International*, everything inside me wanted to die. As I entered Dr. Patricia's office, two women were with her, and she introduced them as intercessors and said they were there to pray.

As I sat down in the chair, I felt I had entered a courtroom in the spiritual realm. I did not say anything and immediately had a strong sense of the Lord's presence. I wept because I was so sick and exhausted from the warfare, and I had never experienced the presence of the Holy Spirit like that. It was different—there was an anointing and power.

Dr. Patricia asked about my childhood and what I went through in my youth. She then asked me if it was okay for her to pray, and I nodded in agreement. She prayed to the LORD to heal me emotionally from the trauma. After this prayer, she asked me if I was holding anyone in unforgiveness.

I had indeed been holding people in unforgiveness. After the inner healing prayer, and releasing the people I held in unforgiveness, bitterness, and anger, I forgave them. She started calling demons to the surface. Many had names the Lord had previously told me and that I saw in scripture. She asked the demons if they were generational, an assignment, or a curse and what gave them legal rights. To my surprise, demons talked through me and answered her questions about who they were and what gave them the right to be in my soul.

Different generational demons, along with rejection and abandonment, had been passed down to me through my parental bloodline. Other demons used all the abuse from my early childhood pain and unforgiveness. I had wounds, hurts, pains from the past, offense, guilt, shame, unforgiveness, and ties with the occult, where demonic activity was attached.

As she commanded them to depart and go to the abyss, in the spirit, I saw them detach, break off of me, and leave with all their demons.

I remember seeing the occult and the contract of the cauldron destroyed by the blood of Yeshua and His blood cleansing my bloodline. What had been a 12-year journey came to a complete end. I felt like somebody had taken thousands of bricks off my back for the first time. I could breathe, and I felt inner peace. I remember just weeping. I felt the love of God and His Holy Spirit.

This deliverance opened my eyes. Today we are no different than Israel and their sins of going after other gods. Our modern-day witchcraft and the New Age movement are being propelled into the nation's mainstream through media, social media, streaming, essential oils seeped with wild herbs, crystals, enchanted oils for love spells, tarot cards, astrology, third eye, reiki, yoga, balance, and energy, seeking spiritual guides, in hanging on a full moon, seeking mediums, having our fortune read, etc. But we don't understand the severe dangers they possess and the doors we open, allowing demons legal rights to our souls. We seek these things out of ignorance and blindness. We seek love, emotional healing, peace, balance, good luck, or power.

There is a Bible scripture the Lord took me to after I became a believer that speaks of God's sure judgment on Jerusalem.

> *"Then the Spirit lifted me up and brought me to the East Gate of the Lord's house, which faces eastward; and there at the door of the gate were twenty-five men, among whom I saw Jaazaniah the son of Azzur, and Pelatiah the son of Benaiah, princes of the people. And He said to me: "Son of man, these are the men who devise iniquity and give wicked counsel in this city who say, 'The time is not near to build houses; this city is the caldron, and we are the meat.' Therefore, prophesy against them, prophesy, O son of man!" Then the Spirit of the Lord fell upon me, and said to me, "Speak! 'Thus says the Lord: "Thus you have said, O house of Israel; for I know*

the things that come into your mind. You have multiplied your slain in this city, and you have filled its streets with the slain." Therefore, thus says the Lord God: "Your slain whom you have laid in its midst, they are the meat, and this city is the caldron; but I shall bring you out of the midst of it. You have feared the sword; and I will bring a sword upon you," says the Lord God. "And I will bring you out of its midst, and deliver you into the hands of strangers, and execute judgments on you. You shall fall by the sword. I will judge you at the border of Israel. Then you shall know that I am the Lord. This city shall not be your caldron, nor shall you be the meat in its midst. I will judge you at the border of Israel. And you shall know that I am the Lord; for you have not walked in My statutes nor executed My judgments but have done according to the customs of the Gentiles which are all around you."'"
(Ezekiel 11:1-12)

We become bait in the cauldron. Just like in the book of Ezekiel, we are in the pot when we allow these false priests who call themselves godparents, psychics, astrologers, healers, etc., to use us as sacrificial bait and offer us as their ritual sacrifices. No wonder I felt extremely sick and tormented, and I had been sacrificed to Satan and death!

Satan's strategy is to remove us from the call and purpose Elohim has for us. He hates us and wants us never to fulfill the mandate on our lives. Yeshua has come to bind up the broken heart and set the captive free.

What took me twelve years to overcome doesn't have to be your case. I encourage you to use the chapters of this book to be healed and set free. Repent and renounce occult practices or any involvement in spiritualism associated with witchcraft. No man, demon, or money can provide you with the peace Yeshua can give you. The Lord will never turn you away and promises to provide you with shalom peace.

Yeshua will return for us—his precious bride, a glorious bride, without spot or wrinkle or any such thing.

–Elizabeth

A BOOK WAS WRITTEN ABOUT YOU

Elohim knew you in your mother's womb, and He saw you being knit together. God knows everything about you and has never left or forsaken you. In Psalm 139, it says a book is written about you.

> *"My frame was not hidden from You, when I was made in secret, and skillfully wrought in the lowest parts of the earth. Your eyes saw my substance, being yet unformed. And in Your book, they all were written, the days fashioned for me, when yet, there were none of them. How precious also are Your thoughts to me, O God! How great is the sum of them If I counted them, they would be more in*

number than the sand. When I awake, I am still with You." (Psalm 139:15-16)

One might think, "There is no way God could use me or my life. I have been through so much. You don't know how bad things were for me."

I know how hard life can be, but like Elizabeth's life, God turned it all around. Now she is ministering in her life's call and purpose.

CHAPTER TWO

Bind Up the Broken Heart To Set the Captive Free

Yeshua said we would have rivers of living water flow out of our hearts. *"On the last day, that great day of the feast, Jesus stood and cried out, Saying, "If anyone thirsts, let him come to Me and drink. He who believes in Me, as the Scripture has said, out of his heart will flow rivers of living water." But this He spoke concerning the Spirit, whom those believing in Him would receive, for the Holy Spirit was not yet given, because Jesus was not yet glorified."* (John 7:37-39)

The Lord gave me an illustration of a water faucet. He said, "If you have a sink with a faucet coming out of the wall and that faucet is full of rust and corrosion, very little water will come out.

However, if you clean it and turn on the water, it will gush out undiluted." The water in this illustration represents the Holy Spirit.

Your heart is like that water faucet. The hurt and pains of the heart plug it up with rejection, abandonment, a root of bitterness, hatred, jealousy, anger, wrath, resentment, strife, unforgiveness, and fault-finding. If you haven't been healed, these are just a few strongholds that can have legal rights to your heart to keep you in a prison house and prevent the Holy Spirit from flowing through you undiluted.

Satan deliberately wounds us to put us in a prison house, so we won't be effective for the Kingdom of God.

In my previous book, *The Bride of Christ Without Spot or Wrinkle*, I testified about the time I was so broken. I felt bankrupt in every area of my life; emotionally, spiritually, relationally, and financially. I was desperate. That's when I cried out to God in my living room. I felt the sweet presence of the Lord filling the room, and I heard His quiet, still voice, not audibly, but in my heart. He told me my childhood had affected me, and I needed emotional healing. The Lord had me open my Bible; when I did, I was at Isaiah 61:1-3.

> *"The Spirit of the LORD God is upon Me, because the Lord has anointed Me to preach good tidings to the poor; He has sent Me to heal the brokenhearted, to proclaim liberty to the captives, and the opening of the prison to those who are bound; to proclaim the acceptable year of the Lord, and the day of vengeance of our God; to comfort all who mourn, to console those who mourn in Zion, to give them beauty for ashes, the oil of joy for mourning, The garment of praise for the spirit of heaviness; that they may be called trees of righteousness, the planting of the LORD, that He may be glorified." (Isaiah 61:1-3)*

This prophecy illustrates how Yeshua would come to bind up the brokenhearted and set captives free.

> *"So, He came to Nazareth, where He had been brought up. And as His custom was, He went into the synagogue on the Sabbath day and stood up to read. And He was handed the book of the prophet Isaiah. And when He had opened the book, He found the place where it was written: "The Spirit of the Lord is upon Me, because He has anointed Me To preach the gospel to the poor; He has sent Me to heal the brokenhearted, To proclaim liberty to the*

captives and recovery of sight to the blind, To set at liberty those who are oppressed." (Luke 4:16-18)

"Then He closed the book and gave it back to the attendant and sat down. And the eyes of all who were in the synagogue were fixed on Him. And He began to say to them, 'Today this Scripture is fulfilled in your hearing.'" (Luke 4:20-21)

Yeshua wanted to heal me of my past hurt and pain and the trauma I had endured and buried in the depths of my heart. However, He said I needed to go back and revisit what I had been through. At that moment, fear hit me, and I didn't want to have to think about what I had endured. At that time, the Christian church I attended taught me that I did not have to look back at what had happened to me in my past. That was great news for me because I had lived in a dysfunctional home with neglect and physical, sexual, and emotional abuse.

I remember the day I turned eighteen years old. I was in my kitchen; I grabbed the counter and held on tightly, saying, "I made it—I survived! I never have to go back to my childhood again." However, I needed to return to be emotionally healed before I could walk in my call and purpose. And emotional healing is also available to you.

CHAPTER THREE

Erika's Story

My name is Erika, and this is my testimony. My life has been tough. However, I am an over-comer by the mighty grace of God. My story and my healing have been a source of comfort to many women who have gone through similar situations. Even though the story is painful, much good has come out of it.

My life story begins in Mexico, with my mother working as a highly paid escort. My mother married my biological father, a sailor stationed in San Diego, and they separated before I was born in 1970. They were divorced in 1973. After I was born, my mother hid my birth from him for a year. My stepfather, who was also a sailor stationed at San Diego, came into my life when I was 30 days old.

While we were living in Mexico—when I was about four or five years of age—the sexual abuse began. My first abuser was my older brother's friend. He lured me aside while we played hide and seek and then abused me. He made me promise not to tell anyone about it. As a little girl, I could not understand why he had done this to me.

In 1976, after my stepdad married my mom, we moved to California.

My stepfather was the only father figure I knew. He was my hero and everything to me. I loved him so much and still call him "dad." He began molesting me when I was nine.

He began to groom me and bought me everything I wanted. He made me feel special. After abusing me, he would call me a naughty girl and blame his actions on me, saying it was my fault. He repeated this over and over until I believed his lies. I was confused, scared, conflicted, and full of shame and guilt. I didn't know what to do, how to stop him, or why I was the only one singled out for his sexual pleasure. He had seven other children with my mom. Later in life, I learned from my siblings that he physically abused them. He was dealing with huge anger issues, and my siblings also suffered due to these issues.

Once we were in California, my mom got a job working part-time at the local cemetery, and her shift began at four and ended at nine in the evening. My dad would force me to go with him to pick her up from work. While we were waiting for my mom in the parking lot to get off from work, he would molest me. Since it was so dark outside, his actions were hidden. But I was terrified. This molestation continued for several years.

I felt like I had a tattoo on my forehead that said, "Abuse Me!"

In the summer of 1984, when I was a freshman in high school, my life got even worse. I began dating a guy who was three years older. He was extremely jealous and controlling and started abusing me physically and sexually. I had confided to him about the molestation by my dad, and he used this information to justify forcing me into a sexual relationship. He said he'd reveal this terrible secret to my mom about my dad's abuse if I didn't comply. I was so used to being abused that it felt normal for me. I loved him so much and could not understand why he could not love me back in the same manner.

That same year (I was fourteen) my sister and I spent a week with my uncle at his house in Sacramento, California, while his wife stayed with my grandparents and their newborn baby girl. He molested me. I was so devastated that this was happening to me again by someone I trusted.

Distraught, I called my parents that night, and my sister and I were immediately taken out of his home. The next day, we were put on a plane to return home. My aunt questioned me about the incident. She blamed me and asked what clothing I wore to entice him. I didn't feel supported or protected. Then I had to continue to deal with the continued molestation by my dad.

I just wanted to die.

That September, as I was walking to high school, I took a shortcut near a residential area. A jogger passed by, and he kept looking back at me. I felt fear rising within me. My gut was telling me something was wrong. When I got to a bridge, I took a step to see if he was hiding there.

He was.

He grabbed me from behind and covered my mouth to muffle my screams. I bit him and fought him off. I ran to school and went to the main office crying hysterically.

Ending my life felt like my only solution. I attempted suicide that year by jumping off a rock quarry not far from my house. I survived, but I continued to feel like my life was completely unraveling.

While at home one night, I noticed someone peeking through the mini-blinds as I was undressing in my room. We called the Temple City Sheriff's Department to report it that night. When the deputy arrived, I thought for sure he would help me. I wanted to let him know of the abuse occurring in my home. He told me that night that I was beautiful and that he would "get me."

His phone calls began that night—around midnight. Then, he began to stalk me and was everywhere I went. He asked my mom if he could take me to a youth group. I protested, but my mother gave her permission. He molested me after driving me to a mountainous area near my home. I never told anyone because he threatened to kill me if I said anything.

Several years later, I discovered the deputy who abused me was a serial rapist who had assaulted several women while on patrol. The local District Attorney asked women to come forward if they had any information or had been a victim. But I stayed silent because I needed privacy for my new family.

During my teen years and young adult life, my problems continued. Several other men molested me. I could not handle all of the abuse and wanted it all to end. Depression and suicide haunted me all day and every day. I was fourteen, scared, and suicidal.

The time had come to let my mom know all about what was happening with my dad. I began by speaking to the school psychologist. She was a beautiful lady, and I began to trust and grow to love her. During one of our meetings, I confided everything to her. She said that she was required to report this to the authorities. I went to my boyfriend's house and expectantly waited while sobbing in my boyfriend's arms. I was fearful of the consequences. That night my mom was told about the molestation.

I called my mom, but she refused to speak to me. When I got to talk to her, she told me I had ruined her life and could never return home. The pain of rejection was so unbearable. I was devastated. How could my mom do this to me? She was supposed to protect and love me unconditionally. Instead of having my best interests at heart, she turned her back on me at the moment I most needed her understanding and protection.

As I was sobbing on the couch at my boyfriend's house, I saw my mom's friend's car pull up to the house. My mom got out and came to the front porch. I was so overjoyed, and my tears turned to happy ones. When I met her at the front door, she told me she had only come to let me know that the police were on their way to interview me and put me in foster care. She warned me that I would never see my siblings again and that my dad was the love of her life. She asked how I could hurt her in this way. She told me that if I put my dad in prison, the other prisoners would kill him. She again asked me if I wanted to do that to him.

She was using manipulation and making me feel guilty. She forced me to lie instead of sticking with the truth. When the police showed up, I lied and told them I had made everything up. I felt like the family sacrifice. I continued pushing down all of this hurt and pain to try to forget it all.

I ended up getting pregnant several times by my boyfriend. He forced me to have abortions, threatening my life if I refused. During my last pregnancy, I decided to protect the baby at any cost. He beat me, lied to me, and dared my mom to call the cops on him since he knew of my dad's abuse and the cover-up.

My mom complied with his demands and wouldn't help me. I was in the middle of betrayal and blackmail and felt like I had no voice or choice. It was up to me to protect my baby in the womb. I hid since he tried everything to get me to abort the pregnancy and kill me. My beautiful daughter was born—the most precious thing in my life. I finally had someone for whom to live and fight. God used my precious baby girl to prod me to fight for my destiny.

As far back as I can remember, I have always loved God. Throughout all of the abuse, I kept attending church. While I was enduring abuse by my dad, I stole a cassette tape that belonged to him. On it was a song by Amy Grant entitled "My Father's Eyes." I loved that song and sang it all the time, and I had no idea it was about God.

Eventually, after attending many churches, I found *Without Spot or Wrinkles Ministry International* in La Verne, California. The teachings and ministry conferences helped me in so many ways. Boot Camp Basic Training taught me that I needed inner healing and deliverance because my mom had been a prostitute and passed down generational curses that had given the demons of molestation legal rights to molest me. Through the power of the Holy Spirit and inner healing, I could forgive everyone who hurt and betrayed me. I hold no anger or bitterness toward anyone. Jesus has healed me and set me free.

When my dad was older, he was involved in a significant car accident and survived. As a result of my inner healing and deliverance, I could forgive him. I stood by his side when he needed me the most, but I knew only Jesus could help me do this. My daughter's dad died in a motorcycle accident when she was only 19. I paid the funeral expenses because he was my daughter's father, even though he had battered me for 20 years.

The Lord revealed to me that he had been a very broken person who had also gone through a painful childhood. I had no anger or resentment towards him. I had forgiven him as well as loved and cared for him. I wanted my daughter to know that compassion from Jesus is true love. As a result, my parents have accepted Yeshua as their Lord and Savior and walk in His light. I met my biological father, and I am blessed to know him. Some people have mentioned that I look like him and have his demeanor.

I thank God for healing me and setting me free from ungodly bondage. Looking back over my life so far, I know that Jesus pursued me endlessly and saved me with love and mercy. He has given me double honor for my shame and, indeed, given me beauty for my ashes.

—Erika

From a very young age, Erika learned to equate love with abuse. Molested by her stepfather and rejected by her mother, she was overwhelmed by feelings of betrayal, rejection, and abandonment Her stepfather regularly told her that she was a bad girl, and she came to see herself through the prism of her accuser.

Erika stayed in an abusive relationship for 20 years with her daughter's father. That may sound mind-boggling to most people, but to those who have lived with long-term abuse, there is a twisted logic to it. She believed in her heart that love was supposed to hurt; this felt familiar to her, which she thought was normal. She had no voice because it had been muted in her childhood, so she had no clue how to stand up for herself.

Also, having been abused by her stepfather, in her mind, it was important not to expose her daughter to the same broken-home dynamic. That was the primary driving force for making her abusive and dysfunctional relationship work, even though it was killing her.

As with many who live in abusive circumstances, Erika turned inward and experienced severe depression, hopelessness, and even suicidal thoughts. She was dealing with ongoing abuse and, in many ways, post-traumatic stress disorder (PTSD). Her heart was broken, and she was utterly devastated.

The mention of PTSD may surprise some, but it's not a diagnosis for soldiers alone. Anyone who has had trauma, been violated, lived in abusive situations, or has fought to stay alive can experience PTSD.

Although Erika had been a Christian for many years, it wasn't till she started attending the teaching of our Basic Bootcamp training, Where the Holy Spirit began His incredible healing and deliverance work. She went to the altar many times for prayer; God met her there every time.

God was healing Erika and restoring her life. This experience was so powerful and profound that she began to experience compassion for her stepfather—arguably the person most responsible for her lifelong downward spiral. She never actually had hateful feelings toward him but felt dirty on the inside and consumed with guilt and shame. However, in time, she was able to go to her stepfather and speak to him about the Lord and how He had healed her. As he started to see the radiance in her life because of God's glory and how she had changed, it impacted him.

All the while, Erika was experiencing more inner healing through our office with one-on-one counseling. She continued to minister to her stepfather, and eventually, he said, "What do I need to do?" He came to our ministry, started to attend services, and the Holy Spirit worked on him in such a powerful way. He knew Erika had forgiven him by this time, but he could not forgive himself.

As her stepfather began to heal physically and spiritually, he was able to receive forgiveness from the Lord as he repented of his sins. Both of Erika's parents have received the Lord through her testimony. Now Erika is walking in her call and purpose as she ministers to so many people. She has an evangelistic anointing on her life.

God keeps His promises and has seen every tear you've cried. The fact that you are reading this book is a divine appointment from your Heavenly Father, and He wants you healed, restored, and sanctified.

CHAPTER FOUR

Puss Pockets and Trigger Events

Have you ever heard someone say, "So and so knows how to push my buttons?" Whenever someone pushes down on our emotional hurts and pains, which we've kept pushing down as a survival mechanism, it can bring up a lot of emotions. These hurts, and pains are what I call *puss pockets.* Why do I say this? Because when you have a puss-filled sore on your arm, you'll cry out in pain if someone barely touches that area.

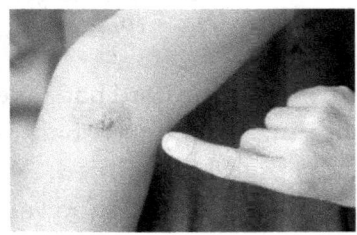

An event or memory that brings up past emotional hurt or pain is called a *trigger event*. This trigger event will result in an extreme emotional outburst. You might get angry, depressed, fearful, anxious, feel like you want to run away, and maybe even become suicidal. You might not have a conscious memory of the hurt, pain, or trauma you have endured because many of us have learned to detach from it emotionally. However, you do feel extremely emotional. It reminds me of a volcanic explosion bubbling up and erupting inside you. You're not sure what's happening.

HAS THIS EVER HAPPENED TO YOU?

When God starts healing you, He does it one layer at a time because he knows how much you have been through. He slowly pulls back the layers like on an onion. I believe He allows circumstances in your life that press into these areas of pain to bring these hurts to the surface.

> *"In the same way that gold and silver are refined by fire, the Lord purifies your heart by the tests and trials of life." (Proverbs 17:3 TPT)*

After the Lord had taken me through emotional healing, I thought I had dealt with all the painful memories I had buried.

Then a situation arose between Reverend Benjamin and me over grapes. Due to the pregnancy with our daughter Michelle and my extra weight gain, I was watching what I ate. One day I got grapes out of the refrigerator, thinking this was a good choice. Reverend Benjamin came in and asked, "What are you eating?"

I answered, "Grapes, would you like some?"

Sarcastically, he said, "No, not now, you and the kids eat everything good in the house, and I don't get anything. How long have we had grapes?"

I said, "Since I went shopping."

He asked, "Why didn't you tell me we had grapes?"

I was confused, and I did not know how to answer him. I started feeling upset and very angry.

As a child, I would not be able to talk when I would get hurt emotionally. Growing up, I had no "voice" –it would feel like I had the wind knocked out of me. Reverend Benjamin constantly encouraged me to talk to him and let him know how I felt. But, at this time, I said, "I didn't like how you talked to me, it was very hurtful." I was so relieved that I was able to share my feelings.

But it did not go the way I thought it should. Again, in a sarcastic voice, he said, "How do you think I feel? I give you money for food, and I don't get anything good. You do not think about me."

That was it! What he said was not valid. I became outraged. I was spitting fire. I shuffled my hugely pregnant body upstairs, thinking, "That's it, tomorrow I am moving out and getting a job. I will never take any of his money again." It didn't matter that I was seven and a half months pregnant, and it was a high-risk pregnancy.

As the anger raged inside me, I asked the Lord what was causing all this emotion. The Lord quickly had me recall a situation when I was a little girl of maybe three or four years of age. One day three of my siblings and I were sitting on the floor eating a bag of potato chips, a rare treat for us. Due to my parents' alcoholism, there was little money for our basic needs. My mother stood over us, yelling, "You little pigs, you eat everything in this house." When the Lord brought this to my memory, I started crying. I cried for forty-five minutes as the memory surfaced. I could not believe there was more to be healed. There was so much emotional pain attached to that memory, and I did not remember this incident until that night.

However, throughout my life, it would upset me when someone would make a rude remark about someone eating. It would infuriate me if anyone made fun of someone eating a lot. I never thought about these emotional responses, they were normal to me.

That night after the Lord healed that painful memory, all my anger toward Reverend Benjamin was gone; I had such sweet peace. I asked the Lord why He had not healed me all at once. He said, "You could not have taken all of the pain surfacing all at one time. You just cried for forty-five minutes from this one memory. Your heart could not have handled all the hurt all at once." This revelation caused me to fall into a deep sleep.

The following day, when I awoke, Reverend Benjamin was already downstairs. I went to where he was sitting at the kitchen table. I shared with him what the Lord had revealed and healed me of the night before. He took me in his arms, held me close, and said, "I am so sorry, sweetheart. I knew you had it bad growing up, but I did not know how bad it was." I told him, "I know why so many people get divorced. They have hurts and pains, which haven't been healed."

> *"That He who has begun a good work in you will complete it until the day of Jesus Christ." (Philippians 1:6)*

SOMETIMES THINGS HAVE HAPPENED TO US THAT WERE TRAUMATIC BUT NOT ABUSIVE AS IN MARY'S ROAD TO RECOVERY.

The healing process from any hurtful trauma or painful event is not quick but must be dealt with one layer at a time. My healing journey so far has been longer than ten years with the expert help of Dr. Patricia Venegas at W.O.S.O.W. Ministries International. Here's my ongoing story in my quest for inner healing.

About two years ago, I began to delve into the effect past traumas have had on my life. I realized that past traumas and/or difficult memories must be exposed and examined before any true healing can occur because traumas are hurts that have been deeply buried in our soul realm. I questioned the Lord regarding some recurring dreams I'd had and asked Him about their meaning. I inquired of the Holy Spirit about past events that had surfaced. I truly desired deep healing and prayed to the Holy Spirit for exposure so that I could be healed. This was when buried memories began to emerge.

I then began to make a list of past traumatic events. The painful memories were allowed to flow, and I definitely felt the buried emotions tied to those events. The Lord then revealed to me that I still retained some trapped emotions from unhealed traumas, which were not allowing me to be fully healed.

Before discussing the traumatic event I endured, I'd like to provide some family background information. My parents, their ten children, my grandparents, and my extended family lived in a small village in Mexico. When I was three, my parents, three younger brothers, and my eldest sister left Mexico for a better life in the U.S.A. They planned to eventually bring us children together to live in the U.S.A. The remaining children, ages four to fourteen, were left behind to live with my grandparents. When I was four, my parents arranged to transport me to the U.S.A. with family friends I'd never met; this is when my traumas began.

When I was taken from my small village in Mexico to board the bus to Mexico City with this couple, all I recall was the wailing of my grandmother and family as we left. The only memory I remember of my grandmother is her sobbing uncontrollably; this was the last time I saw that side of my family for several years. After the bus trip from the village, we boarded the train to the U.S.A. from Mexico City. During this two-to-three-day train trip, I do recall getting physically sick. The lovely couple bought me a red teddy bear to solace me, and I clung to it as my only means of comfort. I was eventually reunited with my parents, but many unanswered questions bothered me for years.

I kept wondering, "What's next? Will I ever feel safe?" Why was I feeling so abandoned? Fear, worry, and anxiety settled into my little four-year-old heart and made its home there for decades. My recurring nightmares of traveling alone and not feeling safe or prepared made more sense to me now. The four-year-old in me needed to know she was safe, and that the Lord had always been with her. Even though there are many gaps in this story, I am confident that the Holy Spirit only led me to the areas that were absolutely necessary for my inner healing.

—Mary

CHAPTER FIVE
Emotional Healing

The term *Inner Healing* is a modern reference to emotional healing from the Holy Spirit. This process involves using the power of prayer and God's Word to deal with the deepest wounds in our hearts.

As believers, we can allow our Father access to the deep hurts and pains. He can take away the pain and heal us. Your memory is not erased, nor does it change your personal history; however, it brings comfort from the Holy Spirit to your emotional pain.

Just as Christ suffered for you at Calvary, inner healing will enable you to have compassion and prepare you to minister to all who have likewise suffered, *"Blessed be the God and Father of our Lord*

Jesus Christ, the Father of mercies and God of all comfort, who comforts us in all our tribulation, that we may be able to comfort those who are in any trouble, with the comfort with which we ourselves are comforted by God. For as the sufferings of Christ abound in us, so our consolation also abounds through Christ." (2 Corinthians 1:3-5)

When Yeshua shed His blood, He carried our inner pain and wounds. *"Surely, he hath borne our griefs, and carried our sorrows (grief, pain, affliction): yet we did esteem him stricken, smitten of God, and afflicted. But he was wounded for our transgressions, he was bruised for our iniquities: the chastisement of our peace was upon him; and with his stripes we are healed."* (Isaiah 53:4-5)

The word "sorrows" in this passage, translates to grief, pain, or affliction.

ONE MIGHT WONDER, "WHAT DO I NEED TO DO IN ORDER TO GET EMOTIONALLY HEALED?"

To begin with, set quiet time aside and pray. During your prayer time, give the Lord permission to heal you. Allow Him access to those areas hidden inside of you.

> **Prayer:** *Heavenly Father, Your Word says You have come to bind up the broken heart and set the captive free. I permit You to bring up anything painful I have buried and ask that You heal me*

emotionally. Please, cleanse my wounds with living water from under Your throne, and I ask for the healing virtue from Calvary to heal all the hurt and pain I have pushed down. In Yeshua's name, Amen.

You may not even remember some situations that have caused you hurt and pain. However, trust the Holy Spirit to reveal these areas as you seek your healing.

Writing about your childhood or past is one way to let the memories, pain, and emotions surface so they can heal. As you begin to write, you may want to do this in stages by asking yourself questions about your timeline.

Start with your conception—that's right, conception! In the beginning, as embryos, it's a scientific fact that we absorb our mother's emotions. If you know, write down what was happening in your parent's life at the time of your conception. If you don't know and have a relationship with them, you may want to ask them what was happening in their lives when you were conceived.

Ask yourself questions such as what was it like growing up? How did your parents treat you? Were they loving or abusive? Were your parents even in your life? Where were you raised? In what order are you among your siblings? What were they like? How did your extended family members treat you? Were you ever abused physically, emotionally, or sexually, and by whom? etc. While writing, if emotional pain comes up, stop, close your eyes, and ask the Lord to heal that area. It can be very emotional and painful. It is okay to cry.

I want you to picture Yeshua standing there beside you, feeling the hurt and suffering that you went through in the past and what you're going through in the present. He has never left nor forsaken you and has always been with you.

> *Prayer:* Father, would You please heal this hurt, and the pain I have in my heart? I give it to You; You bore my griefs and carried my sorrows, suffering, pain, and affliction. I apply the blood of Yeshua to this wound. I ask You Holy Spirit that You would fill this area with Your presence. In Yeshua's name, Amen.

REMEMBER THE PUSS POCKETS

Many times, what you're dealing with today is not about today. Often, it's about your yesterday, as in my case with Reverend Benjamin. You might have buried hurt and pain that you are unaware of; situations in your life may cause a lot of emotions, such as feelings of rejection, abandonment, betrayal, anger, fear, and anxiety. Remember that these emotions could be connected to *puss pockets*.

WHAT TO DO WHEN THIS HAPPENS

Go somewhere you can be alone with the Lord. Ask God where all these emotions are coming from; be still and let him show you if these emotions are connected to a puss pocket. If He brings up a memory from your past, as He did in me, let Him go in and heal it. You may feel like crying, do not stop the tears, as this is a part of healing. Let your tears come as the emotions surface.

> ***Prayer:*** *Father, show me where these emotions are coming from; is it something from my past? (If He shows you any memories, give them to Him.) Please heal this area of my life. I give it to You since Your blood was shed for the atonement of our sins and our healing. By your stripes, I am healed. In Yeshua's name, Amen*

CHAPTER SIX

Accepted, and Loved In the Beloved

Have you ever felt rejected or abandoned? If you have, you are not alone. After years of counseling, I believe 95 percent of the people I have worked with feel rejected and abandoned, many even from their mother's womb.

One of the strategies that Satan uses to wound our hearts is to work through rejection and abandonment. When we feel rejected, we put walls around our hearts, so we won't get hurt. This is to keep love from coming in and love from going out. We might say things like, "No one wants me...I will never love again...No one will ever get my heart... They will never hurt me again..." Satan knows the more love we have, the more faith we have.

Rejection also undermines, breaks, or prevents normal and harmonious relationships between family members, spouses, fellow believers, coworkers, and friends. We might behave in ways that cause people to reject or avoid us.

The Symptoms of Rejection are: You don't feel loved, can't feel accepted, or give love, have self–rejection, feeling abandoned, feeling starved for love, self-hatred, feeling worthless, fear of rejection, feeling defeated, feel emotional torment, low self-esteem, feeling insecure, having a withdrawn personality, seeking to please others, seek approval, internal hurt/pain, being depressed, and engaging in self-defeating actions.

MY FIRST ENCOUNTER WITH A DEMON MANIFESTATION

At a women's conference, I ran into a friend who invited me to sit at her table during lunch. She introduced me to her niece, and she and I started talking. Within minutes tears rose in her eyes, and the tears became uncontrollable.

We then moved to a private room where she started pouring her heart out to me. She confessed she had never been able to love or receive love her whole life. She did not love her husband or five children, even though they were terrific. She wanted to feel her husband's love and love him back, but she could not. She thought it was unfair to him to stay married.

Listening to how painful this was for her, compassion overwhelmed me. I sensed that the Lord wanted me to pray for her heart to be healed so she could love her family. As soon as I started praying for her, a demon surfaced. Her voice changed, her face contorted, and the demon started screaming at me to shut up. It said it wasn't going to let her heart go. The Holy Spirit had me tell the demon to shut up and not talk to me "in the name of Jesus." As I did, she pressed her lips together tight, and her head violently shook back and forth as if to say "no." The demon could no longer speak.

After that weekend, I continued to minister to her. Another demon manifested in one of our sessions when I began praying for her. She slumped out of the chair, slithered onto the floor, and the demon growled. I commanded it to leave, but it would not leave her.

I started praying for the Lord to show me how to pray for her. He gave me a vision of her as a baby in a crib, crying hysterically for hours for her mommy, but she never came. She had neither memory nor words to express what had happened to her.

The Lord had me sit on the floor with her. As I held her in my arms, rocking her, I sang the song "Jesus Loves Me." I prayed for that time in her life, when she was a baby, for Yeshua to heal the emotional pain and rejection. When I did, the demon that had put walls up around her heart lost power over the emotional pain of rejection. The Lord told me many people have no memory of what happened to them before two or three years of age. However, from the time they are conceived to between two and three years of age, what they experienced can affect and throw them off balance for the rest of their lives. Many have no idea why they do or act in specific ways.

When God started to heal me of all the rejection in my life, He showed me this scripture, *"Blessed be the God and Father of our Lord Jesus Christ, who has blessed us with every spiritual blessing in the heavenly places in Christ. Just as He chose us in Him before the foundation of the world, that we should be holy and without blame before him in love: having predestined us to adoption as sons by Jesus to himself, according to the good pleasure of his will, to the praise of the glory of his grace, by which he has made us accepted in the beloved."* (Ephesians 1:3-6)

I must have read it a hundred times. I was accepted and adopted by my heavenly Father. The realization was if God loved and accepted me, it didn't matter who rejected me.

Every time you start feeling rejected or abandoned, remember this is a strategy that Satan uses to keep love from you. You are not rejected but accepted in the beloved.

> ***Prayer:*** *Father, Your Word says I am accepted in the beloved. Thank You that I am not rejected but adopted and loved. If You, the King of the universe,*

accept me, it doesn't matter if no one else does. Please fill my heart with Your love. Give me enabling grace to love You with all of my heart and love others as myself. You spirit of rejection and abandonment, Your loveless power over me is destroyed today; you and every demon in your cadre will depart from me. You will take the walls down around my heart, keeping love from coming in and love from going out. Depart, go to the abyss. In Yeshua's name, Amen.

FOR GOD SO LOVED THE WORLD

The Kingdom of God is all about love; everything the Lord does is wrapped in love.

> *"For God so loved the world that He gave His only begotten Son, that whoever believes in Him should not perish but have everlasting life. For God did not send His Son into the world to condemn the world, but that the world through Him might be saved." (John 3:16-17)*

Yeshua was questioned about what the greatest commandment in the law was, *"Then one of them, a lawyer, asked Him a question, testing Him, and saying, "Teacher, which is the great commandment in the law? "Jesus said to him, "'You shall love the Lord your God with all your heart, with all your soul, and with all your mind.' This is the first and great commandment. And the second is like it: 'You shall love your neighbor as yourself.' On these two commandments hang all the Law and the Prophets."* (Matthew 22:35-40)

How can we love God with all our hearts and others as ourselves if we have walls around our hearts to stop love from coming in or going out?

Love is the greatest gift you can have. *"Though I speak with the tongues of men and of angels, but have not love, I have become sounding brass or a clanging cymbal. And though I have the gift of prophecy, and understand all mysteries and all knowledge, and though I have all faith, so that I could remove mountains, but have not love, I am nothing. And though I bestow all my goods to feed the poor, and though I give my body to be burned, but have not love, it profits me nothing. Love suffers long and is kind; love does not envy; love does not parade itself, is not puffed up; does not behave rudely, does not seek its own, is not provoked, thinks no evil; does not rejoice in iniquity, but rejoices in the truth; bears all things, believes all things, hopes all things, endures all things. Love never fails. But whether there are prophecies, they will fail; whether there are tongues, they will cease; whether there is knowledge, it will vanish away. For we know in part, and we prophesy in part. But when that which is perfect has come, then that which is in part will be done away... And now abide faith, hope, love, these three; but the greatest of these is love."* (1 Corinthians 13:1-10, 13)

> ***Prayer:*** *Heavenly Father, fill my heart with Your love. Give me enabling grace to love You with all my heart and love others as myself. In Yeshua's name, Amen.*

CHAPTER SEVEN

You Have Been Forgiven

What did Yeshua endure at the cross for you to be forgiven and to set you free from the legal right Satan has over you? And how can He give you everlasting life?

After the Passover dinner, Yeshua went to the Garden of Gethsemane with His disciples. He was arrested and taken before Caiaphas, the high priest, and the Sanhedrin.

They stripped and tied Him to a post with his hands above his head and beat Him with a whip called a cat-o-nine tails. (Its handle was about 18 inches long with nine leather straps about 6 or 7 feet long, and at the end of each strap were small lead balls mixed with pieces of animal bone or metal.)

Every lash of the cat-of-nine tails tore into Yeshua's body, with the lead balls ripping into His skin and the jagged pieces of bone or metal tearing it out. The beating caused vast skin strips to hang from His body, exposing His muscles, vital organs, and even His spine. After this horrible beating, they untied Him, and He slumped down onto the cold floor steeped in His blood.

> *"Then the soldiers of the governor took Jesus into the Praetorium and gathered the whole garrison around Him. And they stripped Him and put a scarlet robe on Him. When they had twisted a crown of thorns, (the thorns on the crown were extremely sharp and about two inches long,) they put it on His head, and a reed in His right hand. And they bowed the knee before Him and mocked Him, saying, "Hail, King of the Jews!" Then they spat on Him and took the reed and struck Him on the head. And when they had mocked Him, they took the robe off Him, put His own clothes on Him, and led Him away to be crucified. Now as they came out, they found a man of Cyrene, Simon by name. Him they compelled to bear His cross. And when they had come to a place called Golgotha place of a Skull." (Matthew 27:27-33)*

They took Him up the Golgotha hill, then laid Him on the rocky ground with His open back bleeding and torn. In Yeshua's day, they secured the vertical beam in the ground. Then the accused would be nailed to the crossbeam first, then lifted, dangling as they would drop the crossbeam into the upright stake.

They placed His arms on the crossbeam and hammered five to seven inch nails (more like railroad spikes) through His wrists directly into the median nerve. This caused maximum pain. The crossbeam was lifted to the top of the vertical beam. Yeshua's weight was on His wrists, and His feet were placed one on the other and nailed to the vertical shaft.

The nails in His wrists would have caused His shoulders to be dislocated, causing the muscles to contract and twist. He had great difficulty breathing. If He kept Himself upright, He could inhale but not exhale.

The only way to exhale was to push up with His feet, causing searing pain and causing the open wounds on His back to rub up against the rough vertical stake. Then, suddenly, He couldn't feel the presence of His Father. He cried out, *"My God, My God, why have you forsaken me."* He was crying out to Elohim. He felt separated from God because He took all our sins upon Himself.

> *"Behold, the Lord's hand is not shortened, that it cannot save; Nor His ear heavy, that it cannot hear. But your iniquities have separated you from your God; And your sins have hidden His face from you, so that He will not hear." (Isaiah 59:1-2)*

> *"For He made Him who knew no sin to be sin for us, that we might become the righteousness of God in Him." (2 Corinthians 5:21)*

Then, our Lord said, "It is finished," and He gave up His spirit.

In the days when Yeshua walked the earth, and people owed money, the protocol was very different from today. If someone had a debt they could not pay, it could be humiliating and intimidating. It was not unusual for a notice of the debt to be posted on the front door of the debtor's house, and it would hang there conspicuously for anybody coming by to see. That was quite a motivator. The note remained on the front door until the debtor could finally pay off the debt. Then, they would fold it over and write a single word on it—the Greek word was tetelestai, which meant "paid in full," which was the exact word Yeshua used.

"IT IS FINISHED" MEANT "PAID IN FULL."

At the exact moment of Yeshua's death, the Temple veil was ripped from top to bottom. What was the significance of this to the Jewish people? The Temple veil separated the High priest from the Holy of Holies. Once a year, the high priest would take the blood of bulls and goats for the atonement of the people's sins behind the veil into the very presence of God and sprinkle the blood on the mercy seat.

> *"For the law, having a shadow of the good things to come, and not the very image of the things, can*

> *never with these same sacrifices, which they offer continually year by year, make those who approach perfect. For then would they not have ceased to be offered? For the worshipers, once purified, would have had no more consciousness of sins. But in those sacrifices, there is a reminder of sins every year. For it is not possible that the blood of bulls and goats could take away sins. Therefore, when He came into the world, He said: "Sacrifice and offering You did not desire, but a body You have prepared for Me In burnt offerings and sacrifices for sin You had no pleasure. Then I said, 'Behold, I have come—In the volume of the book it is written of Me—To do Your will, O God.'" Previously saying, "Sacrifice and offering, burnt offerings, and offerings for sin You did not desire, nor had pleasure in them" (which are offered according to the law), then He said, "Behold, I have come to do Your will, O God." He takes away the first that He may establish the second. By that we have been sanctified through the offering of the body of Jesus Christ once for all. And every priest stands ministering daily and offering repeatedly the same sacrifices, which can never take away sins."*
> *(Hebrews 10:1-11)*

With that veil ripped, all of us who believe in Yeshua have access to and a relationship with our Heavenly Father, the God of Abraham, Isaac, and Jacob. We no longer need an earthly priest; we have Yeshua as our High Priest. We have salvation because of what Yeshua did at Calvary—the blood He shed for us.

"But this Man, after He had offered one sacrifice for sins forever, sat down at the right hand of God, from that time waiting till His enemies are made His footstool. For by one offering He has perfected forever those who are being sanctified. But the Holy Spirit also witnesses to us; for after He had said before, "This is the covenant that I will make with them after those days, says the Lord: I will put My laws into their hearts, and in their minds, I will write them," then He adds, "Their sins and their lawless deeds I will remember no more." Now where there is remission of these, there is no longer an offering for sin. Therefore, brethren, having boldness to enter the Holiest by the blood of Jesus, by a new and living way which He consecrated for us, through the veil, that is, His flesh, and having a High Priest over the house of God, let us draw near with a true heart in full assurance of faith, having our hearts sprinkled from an evil conscience and our bodies washed with pure water. Let us hold fast the confession of our hope without wavering, for He who promised is faithful." (Hebrews 10:12-23)

"And you He made alive, who were dead in trespasses and sins, in which you once walked according to the course of this world, according to the prince of the power of the air, the spirit who now works in the sons of disobedience, among whom also we all once conducted ourselves in the lusts of our flesh, fulfilling the desires of the flesh and of the mind, and were by nature children of wrath, just as the others. But God, who is rich in mercy, because of His great love with which He loved us, even when we were dead in trespasses, made us alive together with Christ (by grace you have been saved), and

raised us up together, and made us sit together in the heavenly places in Christ, that in the ages to come He might show the exceeding riches of His grace in His kindness toward us in Christ Jesus. For by grace, you have been saved through faith, and that not of yourselves; it is the gift of God, not of works, lest anyone should boast. For we are His workmanship, created in Christ Jesus for good works, which God prepared beforehand that we should walk in them. Therefore, remember that you, once Gentiles in the flesh—who are called Uncircumcision by what is called the Circumcision made in the flesh by hands— that at that time you were without Christ, being aliens from the commonwealth of Israel and strangers from the covenants of promise, having no hope and without God in the world. But now in Christ Jesus you who once were far off have been brought near by the blood of Christ." (Ephesians 2:1- 13)

Yeshua's blood was shed for the forgiveness of your sins, healing, and deliverance.

"And you, being dead in your trespasses and the uncircumcision of your flesh, He has made alive together with Him, having forgiven you all trespasses, having wiped out the handwriting of requirements that was against us, which was contrary to us. And He has taken it out of the way, having nailed it to the cross. Having disarmed principalities and powers, He made a public spectacle of them, triumphing over them in it." (Colossians 2:13-15)

Yeshua went through all of that suffering because He loves YOU! He paid the price for your sins. Have you surrendered your life to Him and accepted Him as Lord and Savior?

> ***Prayer:*** *Heavenly Father, thank You for loving me and sending Yeshua to die for my sins even when I was dead in trespasses. I surrender all that I am and all that I am not to all that You are. I repent of all my sins and ask You to come into my heart and be the Lord of my life. In Yeshua's name, Amen.*

CHAPTER EIGHT
Repentance

> *"Therefore, since Christ suffered for us in the flesh, arm yourselves also with the same mind, for he who has suffered in the flesh has ceased from sin, that he no longer should live the rest of his time in the flesh for the lusts of men, but for the will of God." (I Peter 4:1-2)*

Satan wants to use the pleasures of your flesh to keep you enslaved to your old habits. The tradition of man and sinful attitudes prevent our transformation into the new person in Christ. We must learn to walk in the Spirit and not fulfill the lust of the flesh.

"I say then: Walk in the Spirit, and you shall not fulfill the lust of the flesh. For the flesh lusts against the Spirit, and the Spirit against the flesh; and these are contrary to one another, so that you do not do the things that you wish. But if you are led by the Spirit, you are not under the law. Now the works of the flesh are evident, which are: adultery, fornication, uncleanness, lewdness, idolatry, sorcery, hatred, contentions, jealousies, outbursts of wrath, selfish ambitions, dissensions, heresies, envy, murders, drunkenness, revelries, and the like; of which I tell you beforehand, just as I also told you in time past, that those who practice such things will not inherit the kingdom of God. But the fruit of the Spirit is love, joy, peace, long suffering, kindness, goodness, faithfulness, gentleness, and self-control. Against such there is no law. And those who are Christ's have crucified the flesh with its passions and desires. If we live in the Spirit, let us also walk in the Spirit. Let us not become conceited, provoking one another, envying one another." (Galatians 5:16-26)

YOUR FLESH NEEDS TO BE CRUCIFIED

Therefore, those who belong to Yeshua need to crucify their flesh, so that they become dead to the flesh, passions, and desires. We have daily choices to live according to God's righteous desires and deny sin, and we crucify our flesh when we choose God's way instead of sin.

> *"And those who are Christ's have crucified the flesh with its passions and desires." (Galatians 5:24)*

> *"I have been crucified with Christ and I no longer live, but Christ lives in me. The life I live in the body, I live by faith in the Son of God, who loved me and gave himself for me." (Galatians 2:20)*

You must respond to the flesh differently than the way you used to by choosing to be a living sacrifice to God and being obedient to Him.

> *"But put on the Lord Jesus Christ, and make no provision for the flesh, to fulfill its lusts." (Romans 13:14)*

When I had to crucify my flesh, in my mind's eye, I could see a fork in the road. I chose to go on one of two paths, the path of my flesh or the way God wanted for me. In the past, I would flippantly make decisions based on my emotions. I would come to this fork in the road, and my flesh would want to take the path of sin, except this time, I would stop and ask the Lord what He wanted me to do, and he would show me He wanted me to take the path of righteousness. I would feel this tug-of-war inside of me. My old nature of sin did not want to die.

The Lord then gave me understanding When I was on the path following my sinful flesh and the temptation of Satan, there were *time-bomb curses* that would go off.

What is a time-bomb curse? There are always consequences to pay when we are in sin. Sin is not for our pleasure but for our destruction. Everything would seem to fall apart on this path since my decisions would make my life miserable.

However, when I chose His ways, He said there were *time-bomb blessings*, and these blessings would come on me and overtake me.

Satan lied to me by communicating that I would not have any more fun if I surrendered all of myself to my heavenly Father. Then the Lord showed me while I was in sin, I was in Satan's territory and out from underneath God's protection. It was as though Satan was taking a baseball bat, hitting me over the head with it, telling me how much fun the sin was and how much I enjoyed it. The truth was sin caused great suffering to those around me and myself.

Crucifying your flesh does not mean that your life will lack pleasure; God is the author of genuine peace that is not tainted with sin in any way. God provides perfect pleasures that bring lasting satisfaction and joy, unlike the temporary happiness that selfish sin could ever offer.

SIN IS MISSING THE MARK AND FALLING SHORT OF GOD'S PLAN FOR YOUR LIFE.

We need to repent of our sins in the flesh to be forgiven. *"Come now, and let us reason together, says the Lord, "Though your sins are like scarlet, they shall be as white as snow; though they are red like crimson, they shall be as wool."* (Isaiah 1:18)

Repentance is so much more than merely being sorry. It's not just adjusting the course but completely turning around (Teshuvah in Hebrew)—physically, emotionally, and spiritually. It is the way to break the demons' power and legal right over your soul. When you repent, you tell the demons, "You will not have me anymore. I've been blood-bought. I have been paid for in full. I choose to come under the full glory of my heavenly Father and to walk in His power."

When we stay in Satan's territory, the sin that we are in hinders us from entering the Kingdom of God. When we repent, we step out of Satan's domain and into the Kingdom of God.

> *"In those days John the Baptist came preaching in the wilderness of Judea, and saying, "Repent, for the kingdom of heaven is at hand!" (Matthew 3:1-2)*

WHAT DO YOU NEED TO REPENT OF?

The following checklist might help, but this is not the extent of evil or the enemy's legal rights over us. As you read Elizabeth's story, she did not know that her family's *traditions* opened doors to demons and gave them legal rights to her soul.

SPIRITUAL BOOT CAMP

PERSONAL INVENTORY CHECKLIST

__Voodoo/Spell casting	__Tarot cards	__Fortune told
__Palm reading	__Acupuncture	__Transcendental Meditation
__Angel Worship	__Automatic writing	__Séances
__Charms/fetishes	__Satanic worship	__Astrology/horoscopes
__Numerology	__Hypnotism	__Table tipping
__Auras	__Witchcraft/Wicca	__Astral projection
__White/black magic	__Pendulum	__Crystal ball/tea leaf reading
__Levitation	__Martial arts	__Yoga
__Ouija board	__Ashram	__Rune stone
__Dungeons/Dragons	__any spiritual belief system that doesn't line up to scripture	__ Demonic shows
__Buddhism/Hinduism	__Demonic games	__New Age/Far Eastern
__Sexual perversion	__Lodges (Religious/Masonic)	__Demonic Music
__Native American	__Spiritual abuse	__Cult
__Roy Masters/The Way Internal	__Pornography	__Immoral websites
__Adult magazine	__Fornication	__Adultery
__Molestation	__Homosexuality	__Violent acts
__Exhibitionism	__Masturbation	__Incest/abuse
__Rape	__Lust	__Prostitution

__Abortion	__Sexual bondage/ S&M	__Bitterness or resentment
__Rebellion/ disobedience	__Critical/judgmental of others	__Anger or rage
__Gossip	__Fear	__Impatience
__Fighting/quarreling	__Arrogance	__Backbiting/belittling
__Hatred	__Lying	__Deceit
__Controlling	__Stealing	__Unforgiveness
__Jealousy/envy	—Drugs	—Alcohol
__Cursing/swearing	_Cruelty	__Pride/self-righteousness

Prayer: *Father, I humble myself before You today. Convict me of my sin and show me the areas of my life that are unpleasing to You. I want to have a change of heart and a change of mind and to serve You. Wash me with the blood of Yeshua and cleanse me so that I would be a holy vessel pleasing unto You. May my thoughts be Your thoughts and Your thoughts be mine. I repent today of all my known and unknown sins (name the sin). I renounce the spirit behind (name of sin). I break every power of darkness over me in the name of Yeshua. I command you and every demon in your cadre to depart from me and go to the abyss. In Yeshua's name, Amen.*

CHAPTER NINE

Unforgiveness

Satan is a legalist, and he knows his rights. Forgiving others is essential to remove the demons' legal rights to your soul and be able to cast them out.

When the Lord started healing me, one of the things I had to do was forgive. I had to forgive my parents for not keeping me safe and to let go of my bitterness toward them. Then, I had to forgive my brother-in-law for molesting and robbing me of my innocence.

When I was already married to Reverend Benjamin, I received a phone call from my ex-brother-in-law. When I heard his voice on the other end of the receiver, my heart started beating fast, and my thoughts began racing. I wondered how he had gotten my number and why he was calling me. He said he had become a Christian and was calling to ask my forgiveness for the harm he had done to me. He had stolen my innocence, and he was so sorry. Then he shared he had been kidnapped as a little boy and molested. The Lord was healing him, and He knew the Lord wanted him to call me and ask my forgiveness. I was able to tell him I had forgiven him years earlier.

When Satan gets you into his prison through emotional pain, he uses *unforgiveness* as one way to keep you there.

One afternoon, I was ministering and praying for a man, and a demon surfaced. The demon was causing excruciating pain to his back and side. I could not make this demon stop or leave. I felt helpless. I told the demon I had the power and authority to make it go in Yeshua's name. However, everything I said didn't work. After each command for it to leave, the demon would say arrogantly, "I am still here." This battle raged for two or three hours. I sensed the Holy Spirit directing me to ask the demon what gave it legal rights to be here. As I did, the demon spoke to me in a hideous laugh with great sarcasm, "I have this man's heart cut in four ways." The Lord told me this man was holding four people in unforgiveness: his father, mother, sister, and ex-wife. They had hurt him deeply. In the natural, he had every right to hold them in unforgiveness. However, not forgiving gave the demon a legal right to torment him.

I explained to the man that the demon had a right to be here because he held these people in unforgiveness. With this understanding, I took him through a prayer to heal the hurt the four people had caused him, and he was able to release them from unforgiveness, anger, rage, and a root of bitterness. The demon lost its power, and the man was delivered. Praise God!

Unforgiveness brings a spirit of torment, as we see in the Parable of the Unforgiving Servant.

> *"Then Peter came to Jesus and asked, "Lord, how many times shall I forgive my brother or sister who sins against me? Up to seven times?" Jesus answered, "I tell you, not seven times, but seventy-seven times. "Therefore, the kingdom of heaven is like a king who wanted to settle accounts with his servants. As he began the settlement, a man who owed him ten thousand bags of gold was brought to him. Since he was not able to pay, the master ordered that he and his wife and his children and all that he had be sold to repay the debt. "At this the servant fell on his knees before him. 'Be patient with me,' he begged, 'and I will pay back everything.' The servant's master took pity on him, canceled the debt, and let him go. "But when that servant went out, he found one of his fellow servants who owed him a hundred silver coins He grabbed him and began to choke him. 'Pay back what you owe me!' he demanded. "His fellow servant fell to his knees and begged him, 'Be patient with me, and I will pay it back.' "But he refused. Instead, he went off and had the man thrown into prison until he could pay the debt. When the other servants saw what had*

happened, they were outraged and went and told their master everything that had happened. "Then the master called the servant in. 'You wicked servant,' he said, 'I canceled all that debt of yours because you begged me to. Shouldn't you have had mercy on your fellow servant just as I had on you?' In anger his master handed him over to the jailers to be tortured, until he should pay back all he owed. "This is how my heavenly Father will treat each of you unless you forgive your brother or sister from your heart." (Matthew 18:21-35, New International Version)

The fellow servant's master was angry and delivered him to the torturers until he should pay all that was due to him.

You might have felt or are feeling this torment; I have. When I held people in unforgiveness, I would lay awake at night, tossing and turning, rehashing what had transpired between myself and the other person who had hurt me. When I awoke in the morning, that person was the first thing on my mind. Other times negative emotions would come flooding back when I saw the person who hurt me or heard the person's name.

Yeshua shows us a different way of dealing with the wrong done by extending his love and forgiveness. Yeshua became a sacrifice on the cross, taking all the punishment we should have suffered for our sins, and he has freely canceled the debt of all our wrongdoings. We, too, must be able to extend that same grace to others.

"For if you forgive men when they sin against you, your heavenly Father will also forgive you. But if you do not forgive men their sins, your Father will not forgive your sins." (Matthew 6:14-15)

You may say, "But you have never suffered or been abused like I have." You may feel compelled to feel hate, bitterness, and anger towards that person or people who have hurt you. You might have even said, "I can never forgive him or her, I can never forget what they've done to me." It is hard to forgive when you are still hurting emotionally.

The enemy's strategy is to take advantage of your pain and suffering to hold you in unforgiveness towards others to rob you of your peace. However difficult, forgiving is vital because unforgiveness brings a spirit of torment, a root of bitterness and hatred.

SO HOW DO YOU FORGIVE?

Ask your heavenly Father to bring anyone you might be holding in unforgiveness to your conscious level mind.

If the Lord brings anyone to your mind, write down their name and what they did to you. This memory might bring up a lot of emotions. It is ok to cry over what was done or said to you because it does hurt.

Don't rush through this part. Our heavenly Father is gentle with us; He heals us one layer at a time. Allow the Lord to heal the wound behind unforgiveness.

Put your hand on your heart and pray this over the wound each person has caused you.

> ***Prayer:*** *Heavenly Father, Your Word says in Isaiah 61:1 and Luke 4 that Your kingdom message is to bind up my broken heart to set me free. Please heal my heart. In Yeshua's name, Amen.*

Now that you have written the names down and allowed your heavenly Father to heal the wound, I want you to see yourself handing each person to the Lord as you pray this prayer.

> ***Prayer:*** *Father, give me enabling grace to forgive and release (name the names) to You. I choose to release them of all my bitterness, resentment, anger, rage, hatred, and retaliation. I place them in Your right hand and ask that You heal and deliver them. If they're not saved, would You send Your Holy Spirit to draw them to You for salvation? In Yeshua's name, Amen.*

YOU MIGHT NEED TO FORGIVE MORE THAN ONE TIME

Just because you forgive the person or persons today doesn't mean they won't do something to hurt you again. Peter asked how often he must forgive, and Yeshua said seventy times seven. We need to forgive every time we get hurt.

YOU MIGHT NEED TO FORGIVE YOURSELF

You might have a hard time forgiving yourself for something you have done. It's essential to know the blood of Yeshua was shed for your past, present, and future sins. I think of Erika's father; he could not forgive himself for what he had done to Erika.

There was a time in my life after being saved when temptation came, and I could feel the Lord standing in the way. I told the Lord to move, I wanted the sin.

After falling into sin, I didn't want to pray or have the Lord look at me. I felt it was too late, and I told the Lord I had messed up, gone too far, and couldn't come back. The Holy Spirit kept nudging me to pray, and I finally gave in. Then, I had a vision. I was in the gutter, dirty, Satan standing over me, kicking me in the ribs, saying, "You thought that sin was for your pleasure, it was for your destruction."

Then I heard the Lord tell me that Yeshua's blood is for my past, present, and future sins. Not that I can blatantly stay in sin, but the blood covers my sin when I fall. Satan wants us to sin because it separates us from the Lord.

The Lord gave me the scripture of the Parable of the Lost Son. At the end of this scripture, we see the Father was waiting for His son to return. Your Heavenly Father is waiting for you to return to Him.

"Then He said: "A certain man had two sons. And the younger of them said to his father,

'Father, give me the portion of goods that falls to me.' So, he divided to them his livelihood. And not many days after, the younger son gathered all together, journeyed to a far country, and there wasted his possessions with prodigal living. But when he had spent all, there arose a severe famine in that land, and he began to be in want. Then he went and joined himself to a citizen of that country, and he sent him into his fields to feed swine. And he would gladly have filled his stomach with the pods that the swine ate, and no one gave him anything.

"But when he came to himself, he said, 'How many of my father's hired servants have bread enough and to spare, and I perish with hunger! I will arise and go to my father, and will say to him, "Father, I have sinned against heaven and before you, and I am no longer worthy to be called your son. Make me like one of your hired servants." '

"And he arose and came to his father. But when he was still a great way off, his father saw him and had compassion, and ran and fell on his neck and kissed him. And the son said to him, 'Father, I have sinned against heaven and in your sight, and am no longer worthy to be called your son.'

"But the father said to his servants, bring out the best robe and put it on him and put a ring on his hand and sandals on his feet. And *bring the fatted calf here and kill it and let us eat and be merry; for this my son was dead and is alive again; he was lost and is found.' And they began to be merry." (Luke 15:11-32)*

Prayer: *Father, I repent of my sin and thank You for the blood that was shed for me. I receive Your forgiveness, and I release myself of all my unforgiveness. In Yeshua's name, Amen.*

YOU MIGHT NEED TO FORGIVE GOD

Satan wants you to blame God for all the bad things that happened to you. My Aunt Doris' eight-month-old baby girl died suddenly from meningitis, which broke my aunt's heart. My aunt was angry at God, she blamed Him for taking her baby for the rest of her life. You might have had some tragedy that you blame God for, but He is not your adversary. He is for you and not against you.

"Be Sober, Be Vigilant; because Your adversary the devil walks about like a roaring lion, seeking whom he may devour." (1 Peter 5:8)

Prayer: *Father, I repent for holding You in unforgiveness. Please forgive me. Satan convinced me it was Your fault, but now I choose to release You of all my bitterness, anger, and unforgiveness. In Yeshua's name, Amen.*

FORGIVENESS AND BOUNDARIE ARE TWO DIFFERENT THINGS

We need to forgive according to the Word of God. However, we do not have to stay in abusive or unhealthy relationships.

The book *Boundaries*, by Dr. Henry Cloud and Dr. John Townsend, says this: "Learning to set healthy personal boundaries is necessary for maintaining a positive self-concept, or self-image. Our way of communicating with others is that we have self-respect and self-worth and will not allow others to define us.

Personal boundaries are the physical, emotional, mental, and spiritual limits we establish to protect ourselves from being manipulated, used, or violated by others. They allow us to separate who we are and what we think and feel from the thoughts and feelings of others. Their presence helps us express ourselves as the unique individuals we are, while we acknowledge the same in others."

CHAPTER TEN

Generational Curses

A *generational curse* is a defilement passed down from one generation to another. For example, if your mother has been involved in the occult, she has become quite defiled (polluted or unclean) and opened herself up to various demons to enter her. The Bible tells us that the parents' sin can cause that same pollution to be handed down to their children. *"Our fathers have sinned and are not, and we have borne their iniquities."* (Lamentations 5:7)

> *"You shall not bow down to them nor serve them. For I, the Lord your God, am a jealous God, visiting the iniquity of the fathers upon the children to the third and fourth generations of those who hate Me."* (Exodus 20:5)

Not only is the defilement handed down, but also demons move in and take advantage of this; this can happen at a very young age in a person's life (often before birth). The person then goes throughout life struggling with the same bondage their parents struggle with.

I had generational curses from my parents, and I did not know I was battling demons. My parents were broken, hurting people; they used alcohol to numb their pain, and my mother was addicted to legal drugs from her doctors. Both had a spirit of lust, seduction, and adultery; therefore, I fought alcohol, drugs, and sexual sins. Through revelation knowledge, the Lord showed me that I had opened a door for the demons to control the next generation through the above sins I had committed. The Lord has delivered me of these demons.

If you struggle with the same bondages as your parents or see siblings with the same problems, you and your siblings may suffer from the effects of a generational curse.

A woman brought her five-year-old boy to my office one day. This little boy was bouncing off the walls. He could not be still for a moment. I asked the mother what was going on with her son. She said she feared for her life. His voice would change, and he would threaten to kill her. He would get so out of hand her father, whom she lived with, would have to step in and stop him from hurting her.

I have seen generational curses on people whose bloodline has been in the Freemasons, and I felt the Holy Spirit would have me ask if anyone in her family was into Freemasons, and she said, "Yes." Her grandfather and father were both thirty-three-degree Masons. Her father cleaned the lodge, and he would take the little boy with him when he went.

She wanted me to perform a deliverance on her son, but I could not get her to understand that her bloodline had opened the doors for the demons. She would have to repent of her father and grandfather's sins and renounce them. I also felt she needed to leave her father's house. Her father could no longer take her son to the lodge, and she was unwilling to do any of these actions. She brought the boy back a couple of years later. He was worse, and I still could not free him because of the demons' legal rights over him and his bloodline.

The good news is you can be set free and wholly released from the effects of any generational curses handed down to you. You can break generational curses with the blood of Yeshua which is more powerful than any bondage that may have been handed down to you! Once a curse is broken, the next step is to drive out the spirits that may have entered because of that curse.

THIS IS ASHLEY'S STORY ABOUT GENERATIONAL CURSES

My abuse started when I was twelve years old. I'm the youngest of six children. My mother would call me derogative names. She would also hit me for no reason, pull my hair, punch me in the face, slam my head against the wall, and often wouldn't let me eat dinner. She would make me do all the chores, including scrubbing walls. These things happened daily.

My mother would find any reason to fight with me and provoke me, and she always wanted me to hit her back. She despised me and wished I would die. She would tell me, "I wish I had aborted you. Why can't you just get hit by a car and die? You aren't my daughter." Her main reason for hating me was that I reminded her of my dad and because I looked like her mother. She made my life a living hell.

I remember waking up at six a.m. to prepare for high school. Mom would deliberately wait for me to walk out the door. She immediately yelled, "If you even look at me b----h, I will f--- you up!" I couldn't believe she would wake up early to fight with me before school.

It was hard for me to learn in school. Instead of paying attention in class, I would focus on what I would have to deal with when I got home.

When I attended college, she continued making it financially difficult for me. Eventually, I decided to drop out and get a job.

She would ruin anything my dad tried to give me and tell him I didn't need any school supplies or financial support, and he listened to her. She would also tell my older siblings not to buy me anything— adding that she would break it if they did.

At 16 years old, I shut her out of my heart.

I told her she wasn't my mother and would never hurt me again— not physically or verbally. Soon after, the physical abuse stopped, but the verbal abuse remained. She tried kicking me out of the house several times, but my dad wouldn't allow it. She would tell me, "You're only here because of your dad."

When I was 19 years old, I was still living at home with no support or guidance from either parent; I didn't know what to do. I cried all the time.

I hated that she was my mother and would not provide the love and emotional support I needed.

I finally accepted that I didn't have a mother and never would. My heart hardened. I decided no one could hurt me—I would hurt them first. I shut anyone and everyone out of my life. I pushed people away instantly if they showed me even a tiny sign of rejection. My motto was, "You think you can hurt my feelings? My own mother hates me."

I gave my life to Yeshua when I was 26 years old, and ever since, He's been showing me how to restore a relationship with my mother. At first, I didn't want to or know how. Honestly, I just wasn't ready.

Four years later, I "accidentally" walked into a Conference, *Releasing A Jehu Anointing to Take Down Jezebel*. This was my first encounter with *Without Spot or Wrinkle Ministries International* (WOSOW). It was the beginning of my heart being healed.

After that, I attended all WOSOW conferences and church services. I finally had found a place that understood spiritual warfare and someone I could talk to who understood what I had been dealing with my whole life.

I have always believed a demon controlled my mom. As young as twelve, I remember seeing the devil in her. After a one-on-one appointment with Dr. Patricia, God began to heal me, and I sympathized with my mother.

I learned the issue *was bloodline curses*, starting with my grandmother. God allowed me to talk to my mom about her childhood.

My mom shared that her mother handpicked her from her siblings and started abusing her when she was twelve. She would hit and slap her for looking at her for no reason, and she would make her do all the chores. I reminded my mom that she did the same thing to me in high school.

When my mom was 15 years old and pregnant, my grandmother kicked her out. When she was 17, she went to live with my dad, and I later learned that he also abused her. Due to the abuse, she hated my grandmother and father, and I reminded her of them. My abusive relationship with my mom was generational.

My mom told me how my grandmother was also handpicked and abused by her mother. She took the rest of her children to the United States, leaving her behind in Mexico at nine. My grandmother had to raise herself and married when she was twelve.

I can now see how the enemy infiltrated my bloodline, causing *generational trauma*. God's grace has begun healing me, and I am now reconciling my relationship with my mom.

–Ashley

If you have a generational curse, pray this prayer:

> **Prayer:** *Father, I repent of all my known and unknown sins and known and unknown sins of my parents (name specific sins if known), grandparents (name specific sins if known), and my ancestors back to Adam. In the name of Yeshua, and by the power of His blood that was shed for me, I now renounce, break, and sever all cords of iniquity and generational curses I have inherited from my parents, grandparents, and all other ancestors. I break and sever all taproots, unholy soul ties, ancestral vows, and seals. In the name of Yeshua, I now loose myself and future generations from any bondage passed down from my ancestors. I command any demon which has taken advantage of these cords of iniquity, generational curses, and*

unholy soul ties to leave me and go directly to the abyss now, in Yeshua's name. Amen

GOD SHOWS MERCY TO THE THOUSANDTH GENERATION

However, when we obey God's will, He shows mercy to a thousand generations of those who keep His commandments. *"But showing mercy to thousands, to those who love Me and keep My commandments."* (Exodus 20:6)

CHAPTER ELEVEN

Word Curses and Cursed Objects

"Death and life are in the power of the tongue, and those who love it will eat its fruit." (Proverbs 18:21)

The Bible speaks of the tremendous power of words for good and evil, blessing and cursing. God spoke creation into existence and His words have ultimate power and authority. Since we are created in the image of God, it stands to reason that our words also carry power.

It is true that words can bring life or death, healing or hurt, blessing or curses. We read, *"But no man can tame the tongue. It is an unruly evil, full of deadly poison. With it, we bless our God and Father, and with it, we curse men who have been made in the similitude of God. Out of the same mouth proceed blessing and cursing. My brethren, these things ought not to be so."* (James 3:8-10)

Just as we can speak in a way that blesses people, we can also speak curses over people.

There was a word curse on my life growing up; my family had nicknamed me dumb-dumb. I had difficulty staying focused in school, and I believed I was stupid and unable to learn anything. That validated that word curse.

When I was eighteen, I thought, why should I try learning? This was when I began painting. Using oils, I was surprised that I could learn something. The Lord showed me the curse that had been on me since childhood. Through oil painting, the Lord showed me that with the right teacher and the right tools, I could learn many different things. The Lord then broke this curse off of me.

STORY OF BALAK AND BALAAM

As the Israelites traveled through Canaan to the promised land, they were to pass through a particular territory. Balak, king of the Moabites, asked a man named Balaam to curse the children of Israel. Scripture records the story of Balak and Balaam. *"Therefore, please come at once, curse these people for me, for they are too mighty for me. Perhaps I shall be able to defeat them and drive them out of the land, for I know that he whom you bless is blessed, and he whom you curse is cursed."* (Numbers 2:6)

But God intervened and warned Balaam not to curse the Israelites. He sent an angel to block his path. When the donkey saw the angel, he pressed against the wall along the road. Despite Balaam repeatedly beating the donkey with a stick, it refused to go further. Finally, the Lord made the donkey speak, and it said, *"What have I done to you to make you beat me these three times?"* Verse 31 tells us, *"Then the Lord opened Balaam's eyes, and he saw the angel of the Lord standing in the road with his sword drawn. So, he bowed low and fell facedown."* Balaam was ready to curse the Israelites, but God said, *"No. I do not want them cursed. You're to speak only what I tell you to speak."* It was so severe that God would kill Balaam for cursing his people.

Let's look at one more word curse. God destroyed the walls of Jericho, and then He put a curse on it. *"At that time, Joshua pronounced this solemn oath: 'Cursed before the Lord is the one who undertakes to rebuild this city, Jericho: 'At the cost of his firstborn son he will lay its foundations; at the cost of his youngest he will set up its gates.'"* (Joshua 6:26)

Five hundred years later, the word curse was enacted. That is how severe word curses are

> *"In Ahab's time, Hiel of Bethel rebuilt Jericho. He laid its foundations at the cost of his firstborn son Abiram, and he set up its gates at the cost of his youngest son Segub, in accordance with the word of*

the Lord spoken by Joshua son of Nun." (1 Kings 16:34)

HOW TO BREAK A WORD CURSE

Get a pen and paper. Ask the Father to show you if you have any word curses on your life. If any come to your mind, write down the word curses spoken to you. Then pray this prayer.

> **Prayer:** *Heavenly Father, I break this word curse over my life. I pull it up by the roots and destroy the fruit of it. I ask that You bless me. Your Word says I am blessed going out and coming in if I am obedient to You. Your Word says mercy and goodness shall surely follow me all the days of my life. Thank You, in Yeshua's name, Amen.*

Suppose you have used your words to curse someone, then Pray this prayer:

> **Prayer:** *Father, show me where I have used my words to curse someone else in Yeshua's name. Amen.*

Write down anything He shows you. Then Pray this prayer.

> **Prayer:** *Father, I repent of my words and how they have impacted someone else's life. Forgive me. I ask that you bless (_____). In Yeshua's name. Amen*

CURSED OBJECTS

Demons have legal rights to our homes because of items we bring in, such as drugs, idols, crystals, witchcraft books or articles used for spells, anything to do with the occult, horoscopes, pornography, and evil games such as dungeons and dragons—games that promote murder, demonic movies, music, etc.

One day a woman brought her four-year-old daughter to my office. The little girl had a spirit of fear that would terrorize her at night to the point where she would not sleep in her bed. The little girl's father was very upset about this. I asked the mother when the problem started, and she told me it began about a year earlier when her sister-in-law had passed away, and she brought several items home that belonged to the deceased sister-in-law. One night after they brought these items home, her husband got up to go to the bathroom and heard an audible voice say, "Leave my stuff alone!" I asked the mother about her late sister-in-law, and I learned that she had been into witchcraft and was very mean. This is one example of how you can bring things into your home unaware of the legal rights demons have, which are attached to these objects.

When I was a young Christian, right after receiving the Holy Spirit's baptism, I started having recurring nightmares in which I was being chased. The last night I had this dream, the being chasing me caught up to me and grabbed me, and as I turned around to face him, it was Satan. He told me that if I gave him my soul, he would give me the power I longed for. Fear overwhelmed me.

Years earlier, I watched a TV show named Bewitched. The star of that show used her powers by twitching her nose. I wanted that kind of power. I was shaken to my core. I screamed at him, "No, I am a Christian." The next day, I told a mature believer about my dream. She asked if I had any witchcraft books in my house. I said, "Yes, I have one and I do not know how it got in my house. However, I kept wanting to read it, but I have not." She told me to burn it in my fireplace. I did as she suggested. Fear filled my home. However, the Lord told me He was with me.

Some people encounter the paranormal in their homes and contact people involved with the occult to "cleanse" their homes. Satan does not cast out Satan. So, no burning of herbs such as sage, and palo santo, believed to have "cleansing" properties, can eliminate the demons.

Ask the Lord to show you and bring everything to light that demons might have a point of contact with; be still and let Him show you. If He shows you something, you need to get rid of the item or items. Sometimes, you can anoint the article and break the demons right to the object. Sometimes they need to be burned.

The Ephesian believers set an example for dealing with occult items. They confessed their involvement with such sin and burned things publicly. *"This became known both to all Jews and*

Greeks dwelling in Ephesus, and fear fell on them all, and the name of the Lord Jesus was magnified. And many who had believed came confessing and telling their deeds. Also, many of those who had practiced magic brought their books together and burned them in the sight of all. And they counted the value of them, and it totaled fifty thousand pieces of silver." (Acts 19:17-19)

After you have gotten rid of the item, pray over your home and command any demon attached to that object, to leave in the name of Yeshua of Nazareth.

Now ask the Holy Spirit to come and fill your home with His presence.

> ***Prayer:*** *Heavenly Father, I repent for giving demons legal rights to my home and family. I command every demon to depart, go directly to the abyss, and never return. Father, I cleanse my house by the power of the blood of Yeshua. Please fill my home with your Holy Spirit. In Yeshua's name. Amen*

CHAPTER TWELVE
Soul Ties and Inner Vows

What is *Soul Tie*? You may have heard the term "soul ties" before. A soul tie binds our soul, which consists of; our mind, emotions, and will, to another person. You think about that person, and they have won your heart. Your will wants that person in your life.

Most people assume these ties are always negative and the result of sexual relationships. But there's so much more to them than that. Some are ungodly soul ties, and others are Godly.

Godly soul ties are formed when a couple is married. *"The two,"* He says, *"shall become one flesh."* (Genesis 2:24)

> *"For this cause shall a man leave his father and mother, and shall be joined unto his wife, and they two shall be one flesh." (Ephesians 5:31)*

We see that David and Jonathan had a soul tie, *"Now when he had finished speaking to Saul, the soul of Jonathan was knit to the soul of David, and Jonathan loved him as his own soul."* (I Samuel 18:1)

In the demonic world, *unholy* soul ties can give demons legal rights to travel back and forth from one person to another. Through ungodly sexual relations with another person, an ungodly soul tie is then formed. *"Or do you not know that he who is joined to a harlot is one body with her?"* (I Corinthians 6:16a)

THE WAYS UNHEALTHY SOUL TIES CAN BE FORMED INCLUDE:

- Abusive relationships (physical, sexual, emotional, verbal)
- Adulterous affairs
- Sex before marriage
- Obsessive entanglements with a person
- Controlling relationships

Unholy soul ties can also be formed from relationships that are not sexual as well, by being tied to anyone that is ungodly. When I went to Cancun, Mexico, to minister, I met a woman with an unholy soul tie with her mother. Her mother, who had passed away, had been involved in a cult and had been an abusive mother. When I met this young woman, she was a single mother of two. She wanted to receive Yeshua as her Savior. When I lead her through a sinner's prayer, demons surfaced. She told me that as soon as her mother died, she felt like her mother. For instance, she no longer felt like herself when she walked down the stairs. She said her body language became like her mother's. She also became abusive to her children, as her mother was to her and her siblings. After her mother's death, her father started dating a young woman about her age, and this woman was into witchcraft.

When the Lord started delivering this woman, nothing could stop it. I had never encountered someone that had so many demons. One demon after another would come to the surface, and this went on for hours. The best description of this is to compare the activity to the birthing of a baby. Once the baby starts exiting the womb, nothing can stop it. In the same manner, the demons were surfacing. The Lord was gracious as He gave us *discernment*. The demons had entered her when her mother died because of the soul tie she had with her.

While we were in prayer for her, the Lord revealed the woman her father had been dating was into witchcraft and had put curses on her and her siblings to kill them. The Lord also delivered her of the curses this woman put on her.

I saw this woman on a return ministry trip to Cancun a couple of months later. She was a changed woman and had become a loving mother to her children. What a difference. The Lord told me, "Look at the fruit of your labor. Generations have been changed." Praise the LORD!

ANOTHER EXAMPLE OF UNHOLY SOUL TIES

A young man was a believer who started being tormented by the demonic at night. He went for counseling, and the counselor found out that he had gone to a prostitute, and from that time on, at night, he felt snakes were crawling on him. As they prayed for his deliverance, the Holy Spirit revealed that the prostitute was into witchcraft. He repented, they broke the unholy soul tie, and he was delivered. *"Do you not know that he who unites himself with a prostitute is one with her in the body? For it is said, "The two will become one flesh."* (I Corinthians 6:16, NIV)

> *"Do not be unequally yoked together with unbelievers. For what fellowship has righteousness with lawlessness? And what communion has light with darkness? And what accord has Christ with Belial? Or what part has a believer with an unbeliever? And what agreement has the temple of God with idols? For you are the temple of the living God." (2 Corinthians 6:14-16)*

When ungodly soul ties or unhealthy attachments with another person are in effect, it can bring about a *spiritual control* that can adversely affect your life.

HOW TO BEAK AN UNHOLY SOUL TIE

Take a paper and pen and write out all the names you are unholy soul tied to.

1. If any sins were committed to cause this soul tie, repent of them! Fornication is perhaps one of the most common ways to create unholy soul ties.

> ***Prayer:*** *Father, I repent of my sin with _____,*
> *I ask for forgiveness, in Yeshua's name, Amen.*

2. You should get rid of gifts given to you by the other person in connection with the sin or unholy relationship, such as rings, cards, pictures, etc. Such things symbolize the ungodly relationship and can hold a soul tie in place.

3. Any rash vows or commitments that played a part in forming the soul tie should be renounced, repented, and broken in Yeshua's name. Even things like "I will love you forever," or "I could never love another person like I love you" need to be renounced. They are spoken commitments that need to be undone verbally. As Proverbs 21:23 tells us, *"Whoever guards his mouth and tongue keeps his soul from troubles."* The tongue can bring the soul significant troubles and bondage.

Prayer: *Father, I repent and renounce my vows and commitments I made to _____. In Yeshua's name, Amen.*

4. Forgive that person if you have anything against them.

Prayer: *Father, I forgive_____ (name what you are forgiving the person for), and I chose to release him/her of all my unforgiveness, anger, and rage. I release them to you and ask that they be healed emotionally. In Yeshua's name, Amen.*

5. Renounce and break the soul tie.

Prayer: *I renounce and break any ungodly soul ties formed between myself and _____ because of _____ (fornication, any sin) in Yeshua's name, Amen.*

Now rip up the paper and throw it away.

INNER VOWS

"Or suppose you make a foolish vow of any kind, whether its purpose is good or bad. When you realize its foolishness, you must admit your guilt. "When you become aware of your guilt in any of these ways, you must confess your sin." (Leviticus 5:4-5, NLT)

An *inner vow* is a determination we make as children and is usually forgotten. These seem even more potent than the ones we've made as adults;

they have more than psychological power; they also have spiritual power. When we made those vows, our enemy, the devil, worked hard to make those negative words come true.

> An inner vow is like telling yourself how things will be.

Some examples are:
"I will never do that again."
"I will never be like my mother."
"I will never allow that in my house."

Remember, in Elizabeth's story, she made an inner vow. "Immediately, I felt unprotected, betrayed, unloved, unworthy, and angry. I made an inner vow never again to tell anyone anything that was happening to me or trust anyone."

Once, I was praying for a woman when a demon manifested, whose legal right existed because of an inner vow. Her father was verbally abusive and always told her she would never amount to anything, that she was no good. She would go into her bedroom and repeatedly state: "I <u>will</u> amount to something, I <u>will</u> do <u>well</u>, and I will be someone." When the demon surfaced, it told her if she made it leave, she would be what her father said about her because the demon had been the reason for her success. She was a very successful businesswoman, and she feared that if the demon left her, she would be nothing and lose everything she had built. She had built walls around her heart, which caused her to have a stony heart. She also had a lot of pride in what "she had made of herself." When we broke the inner vow, she was delivered.

Inner vows are often challenging to identify and take on a life of their own within us, which causes us to deal with reality in a particular way.

> ***Prayer:*** *Father, I confess and renounce the inner vow _____. I break the bondage of this vow. Heal the area in my heart that caused me to make this vow. By the blood of Yeshua, I declare and decree that I am free from this vow and that I am free to be who You intended me to be. In Yeshua's name, Amen*

CHAPTER THIRTEEN

The Spirit of Intimidation and Jezebel

"God has not given us a spirit of Fear but of power, love, and a sound mind." (2 Timothy 1:7)

When the Lord began revealing that I had the *spirit of intimidation*, I had flashes from childhood as a little girl living in an abusive home. In my house, when someone was angry, people were beaten up. I did not have a voice to express myself, to say no, I don't like that, or to declare when something was wrong.

The spirit of intimidation presents itself in four different ways: fear of rejection, fear of abandonment, fear of man, and fear of anger.

This spirit opened the doorway to set up strongholds in my life. Before we became a non-profit ministry, Reverend Benjamin, a friend named Sue, and I met with an adviser on creating a non-profit. Because I didn't think I could keep appropriate records for the IRS, fear began to overwhelm me. Due to Sue's background in business payroll, she assured me she could keep the records.

At that point, I gave my delegated ministry *authority* over to Sue. I took my eyes off God and put them on her. As time passed, she became very controlling and used anger to intimidate me. The volunteer staff could not understand why I, *Without Spot or Wrinkle Ministries* Intl.'s founder, gave her control over the ministry. They were losing respect and trust in my leadership ability. They would tell me things about Sue that needed correcting. However, I would not bring correction or handle these issues because of her anger and intimidation.

I hated confrontation, and Sue excelled at it. When she would call me into her office to confront me on an issue, I would get nervous, and my stomach would become shaky. I would think, "*Oh no, not again. What did I do wrong this time?*" I hated the thought of someone being upset with me, it made me want to flee. When she confronted me, I would tell her whatever she wanted to hear so she wouldn't get angry. I would say I was sorry for things I never did wrong. I would say yes when I wanted to say no. When I was confronted, my mind would turn to mush, unable to think clearly. I was always searching my heart and praying for God to change me so I wouldn't upset her. I never questioned if she was wrong.

When Reverend Benjamin would confront her, she would come and tell me she would quit if he didn't leave her alone. I worried about what I would do if she left because, at the time, he was working a full-time job and could not commit full-time to the ministry, so I would insist that he not upset her.

The spirit of intimidation is used to silence you. The Lord revealed that, along with intimidation, there was an assignment to cause me to have no voice. If we don't have a voice and have a fear of man, we won't speak the truth in love.

When you don't know your delegated authority and want peace at all costs, you bring confusion and mistrust in the people that God (Elohim) has put under you as a leader. This can apply to any area, not just in ministry, and it can manifest in your home or business.

FALSE PEACE AND FALSE UNITY

I would avoid anything that involved me confronting anyone. I thought it was "unchristian." After all, I was a peacekeeper, walking in love, peace, and unity. I would rationalize and tell myself I was keeping the peace. After all, the Lord said, "Blessed are the peacemakers." However, God showed me that there are false peace and unity spirits. Even though I was keeping peace and unity on the surface, I had no peace in my soul, and neither did the staff who were having problems with Sue. I pretended there was peace and unity because I didn't know what else to do. I would leave the ministry upset. At night I would try to go to sleep but toss and turn, knowing something was wrong and not knowing how to fix it.

In his book *Breaking Intimidation,* John Bevere, wrote, "A *peacekeeper* avoids confrontation at any cost. He will go to any length to preserve a false sense of security, which he mistakes for peace.

A *peacemaker* will boldly confront someone no matter what the cost is to him. He is motivated by his love for God and truth. Real peace only thrives in these conditions. The Kingdom of God is a Kingdom of peace – but it does not come from the absence of confrontation. Yeshua said, blessed are the peacemakers (not the peacekeepers) and *"The kingdom of heaven suffers violence, and the violent take it by force."* (Matthew 11:12b)

There is violent opposition to the Kingdom of God! We can't ignore situations and think they will go away. What we do not confront will not change!"

The Lord revealed that demons were operating through Sue, and I could not have peace or unity with demons. He showed me the demons were laughing at me. One day as Sue walked away from me, the Lord told me the demons were saying to her, "We can make her do whatever we want." It was like a chess game for the demons.

While I was under this spirit, it stopped the anointing that was on my life. I had been walking in fear of man and not the Fear (Reverence) of God.

The key to overcoming fear is total and complete trust in God. *"Trust in the Lord with all your heart and lean not on your own understanding; in all your ways acknowledge Him, and He shall direct your paths."* (Proverbs 3:5-6)

The LORD tells us, *"Fear not, for I am with you; be not dismayed, for I am your God. I will strengthen you, yes, I will help you, I will uphold you with My righteous right hand."* (Isaiah 41:10)

As the Lord started breaking intimidation off me, He had me take the headship back. I had to stand in my anointing and the delegated authority God had given me. Taking the headship back meant I had to quit allowing her to dictate and hold me accountable. This was initially very difficult for me to do because of my temperament.

Not only did I have a fear of man, but I also feared that I couldn't do what God had called me to do. I had never walked this way before and felt like the least of the least. When the Lord was trying to grow me up into my anointing, I ran to man instead of going to Him.

> *"Thus says the Lord: 'Cursed is the man who trusts in man and makes flesh his strength, whose heart departs from the Lord. For he shall be like a shrub in the desert, and shall not see when good comes, but*

shall inhabit the parched places in the wilderness, in a salt land that is not inhabited. Blessed is the man who trusts in the Lord and whose hope is in the Lord. For he shall be like a tree planted by the waters, which spreads out its roots by the river, and will not fear when heat comes; But its leaf will be green and will not be anxious in the year of drought, nor will cease from yielding fruit." (Jeremiah 17:5-8)

God wanted me to be the tree planted by water, but I had become a tumbleweed in the desert. I had to begin trusting God and not man.

Because of the spirit of rejection and abandonment, the enemy can use *intimidation* against you to stop you from having a voice.

Have you ever felt intimidated and felt like you had no voice? If so, Pray this prayer.

Prayer: *Father, I repent of having a fear of man. Your Word says You have not given me a spirit of fear, but of love, power, and a sound mind.*

You spirit of intimidation; I break your power over me. I break the assignment over my voice. Your power is broken. You will depart and go directly to the abyss in Yeshua's name. Amen.

JEZEBEL

When I finally confronted Sue about taking my authority, she told me she never took it; I gave it to her. She was right! I did not know my delegated authority, and I had relinquished it to her. God started showing me that I had been in a spiritual battle for the anointing on my life.

The Lord had me study Jezebel in the Bible. We hear in churches all the time that a person has a "Jezebel spirit." Jezebel was a pagan princess. Remember, Paul told us in Ephesians, We don't wrestle with flesh and blood but against principalities. *"Finally, my brethren, be strong in the Lord and in the power of His might. Put on the whole armor of God, so that you may be able to stand against the wiles of the devil. For we do not wrestle against flesh and blood, but against principalities, against powers, against the rulers of the darkness of this age, against spiritual hosts of wickedness in the heavenly places".* (Ephesians 6:9-12)

The Principality that operated through Jezebel is Ashtoreth. Astarte/Ashtoreth is the Queen of Heaven to whom the Canaanites burned offerings and poured libations (Jeremiah 44). Ashtoreth, the goddess of war and sex, maternity, and fertility. Prostitution was a religious rite in the service of this goddess. *Westminster Dictionary of the Bible art.*

King Ahab of Israel did evil in the sight of the Lord, more evil than all the other Kings of Israel, because he took Jezebel in marriage and went on to serve Baal. Jezebel fed the prophets of Baal and

Ashtoreth at her table. (Judges 10:12, I Kings 11:5, 33; I Kings 16:31, II Kings 23:13)

Satan was sitting on the throne of Israel through this woman, through whom demons operated.

This *Principality* targets those with a high call and purpose to further the Kingdom of God. This Principality is gender-neutral, and it can operate through males or females. In Juanita Bynum's book, "Your Spiritual Inheritance," she explains how Ashtoreth can change its gender.

We have read about Elijah, the great prophet with a call and purpose to take down Ahab and Jezebel. Despite all that he had accomplished as an anointed man of God, Jezebel intimidated him. He became depressed and hopeless, which caused him not to complete his call and purpose.

SATAN IS AFTER YOUR CALL AND PURPOSE

This principality uses anger and manipulation to control you. It has a deep hatred of actual spiritual authority and uses anything to gain control of this authority.

You might be or have been attacked by an *Ashtoreth* spirit. When the spirit attacks you, it comes next to you subtly. Here are some ways to help you discern this spirit.

Many people today would call it narcissism. It operates in pride and arrogance and doesn't like to be told no. It will use intimidation and anger to control you.

If you try to confront it on a subject or an issue, it will use what I call "red herrings." It will not deal with the problem but will start turning the table on you and accusing you or taking the conversation in a different direction. It won't apologize, nor will it repent.

This spirit separates you from family and friends. It often says, "There's something wrong with that person, or it convinces you that you don't need them." It is possessive by wanting to keep you all to themselves. I have seen this spirit isolate abused people, so the control and abuse could continue. It could also use lust and seduction to get what it wants.

It will get you so busy you become exhausted to discourage you. Under this spirit's control, you might get physically sick.

This spirit comes off as very religious because Jezebel was a very "spiritual person." But it's operating in a different spirit. You might start feeling like you're not even anointed; it will use the Word of God against you.

I saw it in a vision in the spirit. It reminded me of an octopus with tentacles wrapped around its victim, sucking the life, and anointing out of them, so they don't have time or feel like praying.

One might think, "Why is this spirit after me?" I am the least of them. The Lord told me I did not know how massive the anointing was on my life.

> ***Prayer:*** *Father, I come before You to break Ashtoreth's control over me. I cut off the tentacles of this octopus that's been sucking the life out of me. I repent of intimidation, fear of man, fear of rejection, fear of abandonment, and fear of anger that's allowed this spirit to control me. I destroy its power over me. I do feel the least of them, but your anointing on my life is not the least, and I thank you for your call and purpose in my life. This demon can't stop it. In Yeshua's name Amen*

What if this demon uses you to control others with anger and the spirit of intimidation?

This demon uses the pains of the heart to gain access. Sometimes things were so out of control in our childhood that we've learned to use anger and intimidation to control others. God never calls us to control other people with anger or use a spirit of intimidation to get our way. The enemy uses pride and arrogance, and pride also hides low self-esteem.

If you think this demon is using you to control others, pray this prayer:

> ***Prayer:*** *Father, I come before You. I repent of allowing this demon to use me to control the people*

around me by using anger and the spirit of intimidation to get my way. I don't want this demon to use me any longer. Ashtoreth, I destroy your power over me; I cut taproots, unholy soul ties, ancestry vows, and seals, every assignment and curse over me. You will depart and go directly to the abyss in Yeshua's name. Amen.

CHAPTER FOURTEEN

Paganism

Could paganism possibly affect the Body of Christ today? While studying Ashtoreth and Baal on Easter Sunday morning in 2005, I was shocked at what I found in the *International Standard Bible Encyclopedia* regarding Easter.

The English word comes from the Anglo-Saxon Eastre or Estera (Eostre is also known as Ashtoreth, Astarte, or Ishtar), a Teutonic goddess to whom the sacrifice was offered in April. So, the name was transferred from the Passover Feast, which was also the anniversary of Christ's death and resurrection.

When I read this, I felt like I had been punched in the stomach. The Christian celebration of Christ's death and resurrection is actually linked to the

Jewish festival of the Passover, not Easter, which is linked to Ashtoreth.

How did the word Easter come to be associated with the festival of Passover? The Babylonian idol Ishtar, known as Ashtoreth, was worshipped by pagan Romans, Greeks, and some Israelites.

Ashtoreth is also known as the "Queen of Heaven," which appeared under several names in several places long before Christ was born in the flesh. Worship of the "Queen of Heaven" involved idols and sun worship.

> *"Therefore, do not pray for this people, nor lift up a cry or prayer for them, nor make intercession to Me; for I will not hear you. Do you not see what they do in the cities of Judah and in the streets of Jerusalem? The children gather wood, the fathers kindle the fire, and the women knead dough, to make cakes for the queen of heaven; and they pour out drink offerings to other gods, that they may provoke Me to anger."* (Jeremiah 7:16-18)

> *"They forsook the LORD and served Baal and the Ashtoreth's. And the anger of the LORD was hot against Israel. So, He delivered them into the hands of plunderers who despoiled them; and He sold them into the hands of their enemies all around, so that they could no longer stand before their enemies."* (Judges 2:13-14)

NIMROD, SEMIRAMIS AND TAMMUZ, BABYLON

When and where did this worship begin?

We trace it back to Genesis and the grandson of Noah, Nimrod, the founder of a false religious system.

It began in ancient Babylon and has consistently opposed the truth of God. Much of the Babylonian worship was carried on through mysterious symbols–thus, it is called a "Mystery" religion.

Legend has it that Nimrod married his mother, whose name was Semiramis. After his untimely death, Semiramis propagated the evil doctrine of Nimrod's survival as a spirit being. After Nimrod died, Semiramis became pregnant, and she attributed her pregnancy to the sun's rays, as though Nimrod had become the sun god and thus had impregnated her.

According to the Babylonian tradition, she bore a son named Tammuz, "Mother and Child" (Semiramis and Tammuz). She claimed that Tammuz was Nimrod reborn, the son of the sun god. Semiramis became the Babylonian "Queen of Heaven."

Nimrod also became the false messiah, Baal, the sun god, a satanic deception of the promise made in Eden of a coming Savior. *"And I will put enmity between you and the woman, and between your seed and her Seed; He shall bruise your head, and you shall bruise His heel."* (Genesis 3:15)

CHAPTER FIFTEEN

Pagan Deities that Come Beside Us

I could never understand why Israel kept worshipping Baal and Ashtoreth when God kept telling them it was an abomination. Jeremiah warned the people of the Lord's judgment coming because of their sin of worshipping Baal and Ashtoreth. We see they did not understand nor obey God's commands.

> *"And it shall be, when you show these people all these words, and they say to you, 'Why has the Lord pronounced all this great disaster against us? Or what is our iniquity? Or what is our sin that we have committed ...Against the Lord our God?' Then you shall say to them, 'Because your fathers have forsaken Me,' says the Lord; 'they have walked after*

other gods and have served them and worshiped them and have forsaken Me and not kept My law. And you have done worse than your fathers, for behold, each one follows the dictates of his own evil heart, so that no one listens to Me." (Jeremiah 16:10-12)

In Isaiah 14, Satan said he would be like the Most High God and sit on the mount of the congregation. (Church is a transliteration for ecclesia, the called-out ones, or assembly.) Through these counterfeit pagan days (Saturnalian, Brumalia, and winter solstice), he has been doing just that.

"How you are fallen from heaven, O Lucifer, son of the morning! How you are cut down to the ground, you who weakened the nations! For you have said in your heart: 'I will ascend into heaven, I will exalt my throne above the stars of God; I will also sit on the mount of the congregation the farthest sides of the north; I will ascend above the heights of the clouds, I will be like the Most High.'" (Isaiah 14:12-14)

Finding out all this information, I wanted to click the delete button on my computer and pretend that I had never read any of this. Then I heard the voice of the Lord say to me, "You have asked for truth. You prayed for Me to give you answers to questions you never knew how to ask, then to let you be able to receive those answers."

I had prayed that prayer, but I did not expect to find out that what I had been doing was pagan, it was not only pagan, but this was a demonic principality that had come in next to me in the ministry to destroy the anointing that is on my life.

After finding this information out on that Easter morning, I felt a lot of emotions. Realizing that these principalities and demons go from one generation to the next caused me to feel sick. They do not die. As spirits, they re-invent themselves. *"My people are destroyed for lack of knowledge. Because you have rejected knowledge, I also will reject you from being priest for Me; Because you have forgotten the law of your God, I also will forget your children."* (Hosea 4:6)

> ***Prayer:*** *Father, I repent of rejecting knowledge. Give me answers to questions I don't know how to ask and let me receive the answers. Your Word says I must worship in spirit and truth. I come against every spirit of deception and lies I have been under; you will depart from me and go directly to the abyss, in Yeshua's name. Amen.*

CHAPTER SIXTEEN

It Is in the Foundation

Everything I experienced with Sue, the controlling ministry worker, taught me that these principalities are alive today. I asked the Lord how these demons could operate in a deliverance ministry. What gave them legal rights to be here? The Lord said it is in the foundation of our existing religious system. Then he reminded me that when I minister to someone, I should learn the person's history.

He had me study the foundation of the church. I found that the Roman Emperor, Constantine, took us from our Hebrew roots and put us in a counterfeit pagan worship system. In 325 A.D., Emperor Constantine officially declared at the Council of Nicene (a Roman decree) that worshiping on the Sabbath and celebrating the Jewish (God's biblical) feasts was entirely prohibited. God instructed Moses to tell the Israelites in Leviticus 23 to keep these feasts; They are the LORD's, this is an example of an antichrist demonic spirit.

Believers in the Jewish Messiah have their roots in Israel with all their customs. To become a Christian under Constantine's reign, a new believer in Messiah had to renounce Jewish rights, laws, and customs. To make an even more defined division between the two sects, Constantine, at this time, declared that Christians could only worship only on the first day of the week. The first day of the week is Sunday, the sun god's day. He further changed the observance of Passover (Pesach) to Easter (Ashtoreth).

Mother and child worship spread all over the world; the worship of the Madonna and child historically began before the actual birth of Christ. Pagan principalities and celebrations were used as the basis for Christmas and Easter Christian holidays. The following of Pagan festivals and occult worship symbols were eventually transformed into Christian days of worship.

The New Catholic Encyclopedia, 1967, says:

> *"According to the hypothesis . . . accepted by most scholars today, the birth of Christ was assigned the date of the winter solstice (December 25 in the Julian calendar, January 6 in the Egyptian) because on this day, as the sun*

> *began its return to northern skies, the pagan devotees of Mithra celebrated the dies natalis Solis Invicti (birthday of the Invincible Sun). On December 25, 274, Aurelian proclaimed the sun-god principal patron of the empire and dedicated a temple to him in the Campus Martius. Christmas originated at a time when the cult of the sun was extreme in Rome.*
>
> *Only in the fifth century did the Roman Catholic Church order that the birth of Christ be observed on December 25, the day of the old Roman feast of the birth of Sol, the sun god. They renamed this day "Christmas."*

Constantine incorporated the birth of Yeshua with the pagan winter solstice, the birthday of Baal (Nimrod), on December 25, now celebrated as Christmas. Thus, we began to lose our Hebrew roots as pagan idolatry entered the worship of the God of Israel.

I have heard, over the years, many pastors say, "We know that Christmas is pagan, but that's not what it means to me. We don't know when He was born, so it does not matter to God if we make it the birth of Jesus. It's also one of our biggest days, with the highest numbers of church attendance."

Satan can transform himself into an angel of light. *"For such are false apostles, deceitful workers, transforming themselves into apostles of Christ. And no wonder! For Satan himself transforms himself into an angel of light. Therefore, it is no great thing if his ministers also transform themselves into ministers of righteousness, whose end will be according to their works."* (2 Corinthians 11:13-15)

Fear and Intimidation tried to come back on me. My first thought was that my in-laws would be angry with me. Then I thought about how my children would react to this information. The Lord reminded me to have reverence for Him.

> *"But I will show you whom you should fear: Fear Him who, after He has killed, has power to cast into hell; yes, I say to you, fear Him!" (Luke 12:5)*
>
> *"The fear of the Lord is the beginning of wisdom, And the knowledge of the Holy One is understanding." (Proverbs 9:10)*

I was so confused. How could I have been celebrating Christmas and Easter all these years and not know that these holidays had Pagan roots? Emotionally I was a basket case once I found out all this information. I remember praying and the Lord telling me that Christmas was a counterfeit. But I kept saying, "I know He was born. The Bible says Jesus was born, but when? If Christmas is a counterfeit, when was His birth?" Within 15 minutes, the Lord showed me He had been born at the Feast of Tabernacles. But wait a minute, what was the Feast of Tabernacles? Which was one of God's seven feast Days. I had never heard of this feast before. What was it?

CHAPTER SEVENTEEN

God's Feasts

God led me to read Leviticus 23. These are called the Lord's Feast days, and he told Moses to tell the Israelites to keep them *forever*. These feasts are still celebrated today and are spread over seven months of the Jewish calendar at times appointed by God.

- Sabbath (The Seventh Day)
- Passover (Pesach)
- Unleavened Bread
- First Fruits Pentecost (Shavuot)
- Trumpets (Yom Teruah)
- Day of Atonement (Yum Kippur)
- Feast of Tabernacles or Booths

God provides a complete description of his entire plan for the salvation of humanity within the LORD's Feasts.

When Yeshua was speaking to His disciples after he was raised from the grave and before He was taken up, *"He said to them, "These are the words which I spoke to you while I was still with you, that all things must be fulfilled which were written in the Law of Moses and the Prophets and the Psalms concerning Me."* (Luke 24:44)

Yeshua also tells us Moses wrote about Him. *"You search the Scriptures, for in them you think you have eternal life; and these are they which testify of Me. . . . For if you believed Moses, you would believe Me; for he wrote about Me."* (John 5: 39, 46)

We need to understand the prophetic fulfillment of what Moses wrote and that these Biblical Feasts are part of the restoration process required to prepare us for Yeshua's second coming.

> *"That He might sanctify and cleanse her with the washing of **water by the word**, that He might present her to Himself a glorious church, not having spot or wrinkle or any such thing, but that she should be holy and without blemish." (Ephesians 5:26-27)*

Leviticus 23 starts with the *Sabbath* (The fourth of the Ten Commandments God never changed. It is celebrated every week, from sundown on the sixth day to sunset on the seventh day. On the Jewish calendar, the day starts at dusk.)

The spring Feast Days began with *Passover* (which is when Yeshua was crucified. Matthew 26-27), the *Feast of Unleavened Bread* (leaven represents sin; Yeshua knew no sin; unleavened also represents sanctification), and then *First Fruit,* (when Yeshua rose from the grave three days after He was crucified. *"But now Christ is risen from the dead and has become the first fruits of those who have fallen asleep."* (1 Corinthians 15)

Shavuot is the baptism of the Holy Spirit and was given to Yeshua's disciples fifty days after Passover, in Acts 2.

The fall Feast days begin with *Rosh Hashanah* (also called *Yom Teruah* or *Feast of Trumpets*. Many believe that Yeshua will return on this day with the last blast, (1 Corinthians 15:52). It is ten days before the day of Atonement (also called *Yom Kippur*)**,** Yeshua is our High Priest, and He took His blood into the Holies of Holies for our Atonement once and for all. (Hebrews 10). The last one is the *Feast of Tabernacles.*

Many scholars believe Yeshua was born at the *Feast of Tabernacles*, based on their study of the birth of John the Baptist, who was born on Passover, and six months later was the birth of Yeshua. As noted in John 1.

In celebrating the LORD's Holy Feast Days, we see how Yeshua fulfilled the prophetic significance of each written about him.

As believers in Yeshua, the Jewish Messiah, we have been grafted into the olive tree, which represents Israel; the root of this olive tree is the first five books of our bible (The *TORAH*); these are not just Israel's holy days but our holidays.

Olive Tree
Roots of Olive Tree

Rosh Hashanah — Passover
Day of Atonement — Unleavened
Shavuot — Sabbath — First Fruits
Feast of Tabernacles

> *"For if the first fruit is holy, the lump is also holy; and if the root is holy, so are the branches. And if some of the branches were broken off, and you, being a wild olive tree, were grafted in among them, and with them became a partaker of the root and fatness of the olive tree, do not boast against the branches. But if you do boast, remember that you do not support the root, but the root supports you." (Romans 11:16-18)*

We are not grafted into the counterfeit Roman tree; Constantine created. The root of this tree is pagan, and it also has divided us through Denominations.

Rome
Roots of Counterfeit Tree

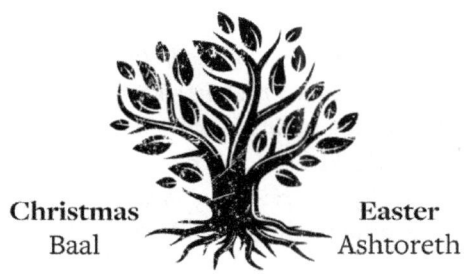

Christmas — **Easter**
Baal — Ashtoreth

Sunday Worship — **Queen of Heaven**
Baal — Ashtoreth

Denominations

"You will know them by their fruits. Do men gather grapes from thornbushes or figs from thistles? Even so, every good tree bears good fruit, but a bad tree bears bad fruit. A good tree cannot bear bad fruit, nor can a bad tree bear good fruit." (Matthew 7:16-18)

We must remember that Satan cannot create; he is a counterfeiter (counterfeit: a copy that looks like the original of something). We are in a spiritual war; we must be willing to align our beliefs with God's Word. We must be willing to let go of anything we deem religious or a tradition of man that is not biblically based.

"And He Himself gave some to be apostles, some prophets, some evangelists, and some pastors and

teachers, for the equipping of the saints for the work of ministry, for the edifying of the body of Christ, till we all come to the unity of the faith and of the knowledge of the Son of God, to a perfect man (mature), to the measure of the stature of the fullness of Christ; that we should no longer be children, tossed to and fro and carried about with every wind of doctrine, by the trickery of men, in the cunning craftiness of deceitful plotting, but, speaking the truth in love, may grow up in all things into Him who is the head—Christ— from whom the whole body, joined and knit together by what every joint supplies, according to the effective working by which every part does its share, causes growth of the body for the edifying of itself in love." (Ephesians 4:11-16)

"Jesus said to her, "Woman, believe Me, the hour is coming when you will neither on this mountain, nor in Jerusalem, worship the Father. You worship what you do not know; we know what we worship, for salvation is of the Jews. But the hour is coming, and now is, when the true worshipers will worship the Father in spirit and truth; for the Father is seeking such to worship Him. God is Spirit, and those who worship Him must worship in spirit and truth." (John 4:21-24)

Prayer: *Father, please give me wisdom, knowledge, and understanding. I do not want to be tossed to and fro with every wind of doctrine nor worship You under a counterfeit system; I want to worship You in spirit and truth. In Yeshua's name, Amen.*

CHAPTER EIGHTEEN

Harlotry

A husband and wife came into my office several times for marriage counseling. When the man would come in for his individual session, a demon would surface and talk to me. It informed me, with a mocking and hideous laugh, that I had no idea who or what it was and that it had a legal right to stay. It was correct, I had no idea what I had encountered. I suggested they attend an upcoming Boot Camp for Marriage weekend. At these conferences, the attendees enjoy teachings, prayer, a dinner, and a formal renewal of wedding vows. They agreed to attend. A demon surfaced in her during the weekend when I prayed over this couple. My team took her aside to pray for her and they asked the demon what gave it a legal right to be there. It said her husband gave it the legal right, and no one could make it leave.

The couple came to our hotel room that night after the service ended. The husband confessed that he was taking drugs and watching pornography. And that he had no plans to stop. The couple met with me for about six months for marriage counseling. During this time, they continued to argue about his illicit sexual activities. He would cease the activities for a while until his wife calmed down. Then, he would start up again, taking drugs and watching pornography. He would also go on weekend drug binges with prostitutes.

At this time, he was attending a *seeker-friendly* church. He was under the belief that he was a sinner saved by grace and that the blood of Yeshua atoned for all of his sins, past, present, and future, so he felt safe continuing in this lifestyle.

His wife finally decided to divorce him. During this estrangement, he said he loved his children but hated his wife. He did not want her to have anything from the marriage. He even mentioned that he would rather burn the house down than allow her to have it.

Because of the upcoming holidays, this couple decided to hold off on divorce proceedings. At this time, the husband agreed to come in for more counseling. Before this session, I fasted and prayed for them, particularly for him. During my prayer time, the Lord took me to the following scripture from Hosea 4:11-14,

> "<u>Harlotry</u>, wine, and new wine enslave the heart. My people ask counsel from their wooden idols, and their staff informs them. For the spirit of harlotry has caused them to stray, and they have played the harlot against their God. They offer sacrifices on the mountaintops, and burn incense of the hills, under oaks, poplars, and terebinths, because their shade is good. Therefore, your daughters commit harlotry, and your brides commit adultery. I will not punish your daughters when they commit harlotry, nor your brides when they commit adultery; For the men themselves go apart with harlots and offer sacrifices with a ritual harlot. Therefore, people who do not understand will be trampled."

In the Amplified Version it reads:

> "Prostitution, wine, and new wine take away the mind and the (spiritual) understanding. My people consult their (lifeless) wooden idol, and their (diviner's) wand gives them oracles. For a spirit of prostitution has led them astray (morally and spiritually), and they have played the prostitute, withdrawing themselves from their God." (Hosea 4:11.12)

The Lord then explained to me that *harlotry* is the spirit behind prostitution (sex for money), and pornography.

> *"How degenerate is your heart!" says the Lord GOD, "seeing you do all these things, the deeds of a brazen heart." (Ezekiel 16:31)*

> *'Flee sexual immorality. Every sin that a man does is outside the body, but he who commits sexual immorality sins against his own body.' (1 Corinthians 6:18)*

When the husband returned to my office for his next appointment, I began praying for him, and the Lord prompted me to address the spirit of harlotry. As I did, the demon arose and was so angry because I knew its name. He charged after me, cussing with rage. The Holy Spirit pinned him against the wall while I finished praying over him. Our Lord is so good. At this time, the couple did not get a divorce but continued in counseling for about six months.

THE PRINCIPALITY OF HARLOTRY IS SPIRITUAL ADULTERY

Although this spirit might allow its victims to attend church services, it keeps them wallowing in sexual sins, thus pulling them farther away from walking with God, knowing Him, and obeying Him. *"Their (immoral) practices will not permit them to return to their God, for the spirit of prostitution is within them and they do not know the LORD (they do not recognize, appreciate, heed or cherish Him." (Hosea 5:4 AMP)*

SOUL TIES CONNECTION

"Do you not know that he who is joined to a harlot (porn) is one body with her? For "the two," He says, "shall become one flesh." But he who is joined to the Lord is one spirit with Him. Flee sexual immorality. Every sin a man does is outside the body, but he who commits sexual immorality sins against his own body. Or do you not know that your body is the temple of the Holy Spirit who is in you, whom you have from God, and you are not your own? For you were brought with a price; therefore, glorify God in your body and in your spirit, which is God's" (1 Corinthians 6:15-20)

When people engage in ungodly sexual activities, they think they aren't hurting anyone. The Lord revealed to me that because a *soul tie* is formed with the person or persons being viewed via varied mediums (television, internet, magazine, books, movie theaters). The demons which are attached to those people within these devices cause the viewer to become subject to the demons, who now have legal rights over the viewer. Mike Warnke, in his book, *The Satan Seller*, mentions that before becoming a Christian, he was a high priest in Satanism and used the money made from pornography movies to fund his lavish lifestyle. He said that the actors used in the film were usually using drugs and alcohol, and many were being used as sex slaves. The under-aged actors had been trafficked illicitly and used in child pornography. Sometimes, bestiality occurred, as well.

This principality allows demons to enter your soul realm. Whether you physically cheat on your spouse or not, it opens the door to the spirit of adultery. This spirit causes you to highlight the flaws in your spouse and allows you to be lustfully attracted to another person.

> *"But I say to you that whoever looks at a woman to lust for her has already committed adultery with her in his heart."* (Matthew 5:28)

LIES CHRISTIANS BELIEVE ABOUT PORNOGRAPHY AND SEX

"I need this." Anyone who has grown accustomed to a steady stream of pornography has been affected by its addicting effects. Although many porn and sex-addicted Christians hate what they're part of, they believe they can't live without it.

"I will never change." This belief is connected to countless promises and attempts to stop acting out. Despite all attempts to cease engaging in these activities, nothing has worked. In many cases, this behavior has escalated beyond any of their expectations. Now they are feeling defeated and hopeless.

"No one would understand." One tactic the enemy uses is to "divide and conquer." People who can't stop acting out believe they're alone and no one else would be able to relate. They believe that exposure would result in other people's rejection.

"My spouse would never get over this." Pornography and other misuses of sex represent a legitimate betrayal of the marriage. Christians discovering a spouse's misbehavior experience severe hurt, anger, and trauma. The addicted spouse often doesn't want to end the marriage and fears that the exposure will result in divorce.

> **Prayer:** *Heavenly Father, cause me to hate sin the way you hate sin. I need Your help! I can't fight these demons by myself. I feel so far away from You, and I want to feel close to You. I repent for turning to the god of Harlotry. I break its power over me. I break every soul tie formed with the images I have allowed in. I break every stronghold over my mind. I command every demon I have allowed into me, my family, and my home, to depart and go directly to the abyss. In Yeshua's name, Amen.*

CHAPTER NINETEEN

Some Spirits Which Cause Pain and Suffering

"Do not allow any of your children to be offered to Molech." (Leviticus 18:21)

SPIRIT OF MOLECH

Passages in Kings, Isaiah, and Jeremiah refer to a bronze statue, a pagan god with a fire inside the figure, into which children were sacrificed

We are in a spiritual war, and these demon gods do not die; they reinvent themselves. Abortion is under the demon god of Moloch, and it gives legal rights to the demons of death, hades, murder, and suicide.

I spoke at a women's ministry, and at the end of the service, I asked if anyone wanted me to pray for them to come to the front. One woman had her 22-year-old son with her, and he wanted prayer. He told me he had been depressed all his life, and the medications they gave him were not working. They kept changing his prescription to find something that would work. As I began to pray for him, he fell to the floor, and a demon manifested. I kept telling the demon I had authority, and it had to leave. But it didn't.

I started asking the Lord what gave the demon a legal right, and the Lord told me the mother had an abortion before she got pregnant with her son. Demons of death, hades, murder, and suicide had entered him in his mother's womb. I asked the mom if she had had an abortion before she got pregnant with him, and she confirmed this. I asked her to repent of blood-guiltiness and ask the Lord for forgiveness. When she did this, the demon in her son lost its power and had to leave.

On another occasion, a woman came to the ministry for prayer because she had many near-death experiences. The most recent was a terrible car accident, which left her with a severe back injury. She almost died. As I began praying for her, I asked her if she had ever had an abortion, and she told me she had several. After I had her repent of the abortions, I cast out the spirits of death, hades, murder, and suicide, and she was healed that day.

Unfortunately, many women have had abortions, which gives these demons legal rights. Many women try to commit suicide after an abortion because of their guilt and emotional pain. The young man involved in the relationship often abandons the woman after an abortion, and most people feel *shame, guilt,* and *regret.*

If you have had an abortion, pray this prayer:

__Prayer:__ Heavenly Father, I repent of my sin of blood-guiltiness. Please forgive me. Please heal my heart. Thank You for double honor for shame. Thank You that my baby is with You, and I will spend eternity with my child. I renounce every demon of death, hades, murder, and suicide; Your power over me is broken. You will depart and go directly to the abyss and never return. In Yeshua's name, Amen.

CHAPTER TWENTY

Drugs and Alcohol

"Be alert and of sober mind. Your enemy the devil prowls around like a roaring lion looking for someone to devour." (Peter 5:8)

I was raised in a dysfunctional, abusive, and alcoholic home. As a baby, my parents would give me a hot toddy when I was sick. Growing up, I was unaware that you could have a good time without alcohol. In our home, it was customary in my family to have alcohol at every get-together and on holidays.

I have no memory of ever functioning without alcohol or drugs. After having my first baby at the age of thirteen, I left my parent's home and was on my own at the age of fifteen.

By then, I was an alcoholic and using amphetamines (speed).

I remember feeling lost and so alone. I would get drunk to go out and sin, then the next day, I would drink to forget the shame of the sinning done the night before.

At sixteen, I moved in with my first husband, and that's when I started smoking marijuana while continuing to drink alcohol.

My journey with God began with my grandmother's influence as a very young child, as she would take me to church with her almost every Sunday while we were living in Texas. Then, when I was six, we moved to California, and I would attend church off and on. Church attendance was a little more regular when I married my first husband. Even though I was attending church, whenever I smoked marijuana, I lost interest in a relationship with God and in listening to Christian music, and my emotions were numb. The Lord then gave me a vision of Satan rocking me to sleep in his arms. I now understand that Satan uses various addictions (prescription and illegal drugs, alcohol, sexual, and technological) to put people into a spiritual state of slumber.

For example, once, while in the hospital, I had to take medication for surgery. Periodically, I would slip back and forth into reality while watching television. I felt confused and kept having to think about where I was. Then the Holy Spirit gave me this revelation. In society and today's church, there seems to be a spirit of slumber over the body of Christ of not being spiritually awake. The Lord also showed me that Satan wasn't interested in this current generation but was going after our children and any subsequent generations.

Through drugs and alcohol, society has opened the door to demons. During the end times, this would allow people to have an easy entry for demons and a way to come into alliance with the Antichrist by taking his mark. (Rev. 13:16,17) *"It also forced all people, great and small, rich and poor, free and slave to receive a mark on their right hands or on their foreheads, so that that could not buy or sell unless they had the mark, which is the name of the beast or the number of its name."*)

> *"But concerning the times and the seasons, brethren, you have no need that should write to you. For you yourselves know perfectly that the day of the Lord so comes as a thief in the night. For when they say, "Peace and safety!" then sudden destruction comes upon them, as labor pains upon a pregnant woman. And they shall not escape. But you, brethren, are not in darkness, so that this Day should not overtake you as a thief. You are all sons of light and sons of the day. We are not of the night nor of darkness. Therefore, let us not sleep, as others do, but let us watch and be sober. For those who sleep, sleep at night, and those who get drunk are drunk at night. But let us who are of the day be sober, putting on the breastplate of faith and love, as a helmet the hope of salvation. For God did not appoint us to wrath, but to obtain salvation through*

our Lord Jesus Christ, who died for us, that whether we wake or sleep, we should live together with Him." (1 Thessalonians 5:1-10)

These addictions keep us from being healed. When I was an alcoholic and on drugs, I self-medicated to numb the emotional pain of my pain-filled past.

Several scriptures address drinking alcohol in the Bible. For example, in Ephesians, Paul writes, *"And do not be drunk with wine, in which is dissipation (excessive drinking), but be filled with the Spirit." "Wine is a mocker, strong drink is a brawler, And whoever is led astray by it is not wise." (Proverbs 20:1)*

I did things a godly woman shouldn't or wouldn't do during my early life. The Lord showed me that when I used drugs or alcohol, His will would be pushed out of my way, and that left room for the demons to have their way. As I minister to hurting people, I have seen these demonic manifestations during counseling sessions. Those affected have divulged to me that if they had a sex addiction, it would start with alcohol, then on to drugs, then pornography. Sometimes they would begin with drugs, then digress to pornography and other sexual sins. The demons of anger, rage, depression, hopelessness, jealousy, lust, and seduction would also surface.

Temptation is nothing more than a demon talking to you, and when you give in to this temptation, you are giving your soul to the demon. *"No temptation has overtaken you except such as is common to man; but God is faithful, who will not allow you to be tempted beyond what you are able, but with the temptation will also make the way of escape, that you may be able to bear it." (1 Corinthians 10:13)*

The more I succumbed to the temptation of alcohol or drugs, I found myself opening the door to forces (demons) that would hurt me spiritually. Some demonic entry methods (not possession in Christians) are through ungodly music, movies, technology, magazines, books, etc. During these times of engaging in drugs or alcohol, I would participate in activities that I would not otherwise allow myself or my children to engage in while I was sober and not "under the influence."

There were times after I had sinned that I felt like I would never be free of sin. The Lord showed me that He desired that I hate sin as much as He hates sin. When I would be overwhelmed with guilt and shame, I would cry out to God, and He would be gracious enough to deliver me from that bondage.

We, as the Bride of Christ, our Messiah, have been set apart for His call and purpose. Drugs and alcohol cause us to miss the mark (sin), which opens the door to our soul realm to become infested with demons. The Lord tells us, "Be holy for I am holy." (Leviticus 19-20) The word for holy in Hebrew is *"Kadosh,"* which means to be sanctified, consecrated, and dedicated. In simpler terms, it means to be set apart for a specific purpose.

If you are ready to become set apart for His purpose and free from the bondage of drugs and alcohol, pray this prayer:

Prayer: *Heavenly Father, I want to be holy as You are holy. I want to be set apart for Your good and perfect plan for my life. I repent for allowing these demons to infiltrate my soul. I repent of my parent's sins back to Adam and renounce every spirit behind drugs and alcohol, which is in my bloodline. I command you spirits to depart from me. Go to the abyss and never return. Father, cause me to hate sin the way that You hate it. In Yeshua's name. Amen.*

CHAPTER TWENTY-ONE

Canceling Satan's Special Assignments and Attacks

Satan sends special assignments against you. When he knows you have an assignment from the Lord to accomplish a mandate, he sends demons to attack and stop you.

A while back, half of the core group of our ministry ended up leaving. This group was strong; they loved the ministry and were dedicated to the anointing. They gave of their time and resources. They were strong pillars in the ministry. They had all been personally touched and had experienced miracles in their lives through this anointing. This group came to me with some complaints.

There was a *spirit of offense* in them that turned to a *root of bitterness*. Soon this group left. We were all shocked. We could not believe these people, of all people, would leave the ministry.

However, one woman from this group continued attending the services. When she came, you could see she had a *spirit of heaviness* on her. She could barely drag herself into the church. She came and asked to meet with me. She was so depressed and heavy. In the meeting, she shared with me how she felt everyone at church rejected her and that I did not love her. Even though every time she came to church, I would hug her and tell her how much I loved her. She said she heard me say the words, but she thought every sermon I preached was directed at her to wound and hurt her, which was not the case. She would leave church more depressed.

As we started praying, a demon surfaced. I asked, "What gave you a legal right to be here," It said it was an *assignment*.

I then asked, "What was the assignment?" It said, "Destruction, I was sent to destroy her." Several demons that night manifested: *rejection, sadness,* and *depression*, to name a few. These demons wanted her and the others out of the ministry. We won that night, and thankfully she did not leave the ministry.

The Lord prayed for Peter's faith not to fail him. Then He told him, strengthen your brother. *"And the Lord said, "Simon, Simon! Indeed, Satan has asked for you, that he may sift you as wheat. But I have prayed for you, that your faith should not fail; and when you have returned to Me, strengthen your brethren."* (Luke 22:31-32)

It is essential to have faith when going through such a trial. We also must be sober and vigilant in our walk. As we see, the young woman at church was resisting as much as she could in the flesh. *"Be sober, be vigilant; because your adversary the devil walks about like a roaring lion, seeking whom he may devour. Resist him, steadfast in the faith, knowing that the same sufferings are experienced by your brotherhood in the world. But may the God of all grace, who called us to His eternal glory by Christ Jesus, after you have suffered a while, perfect, establish, strengthen, and settle you."* (1 Peter 5:8-10)

These assignments can come against other areas such as your homes, families, jobs, etc. Remember, they are there to stop your call and purpose.

CANCELING ASSIGNMENTS:

Prayer: *Father, I acknowledge that You are the ruler far above all principalities, powers, and dominions. I cancel and break all assignments against me, my call and purpose, my family, and everything pertaining to me. I make them null and void and send all assignments to the abyss in the name of Yeshua. Amen.*

HITCHHIKING SPIRITS AND RETALIATING SPIRITS

You may have ministered to someone struggling with depression, and suddenly, you are depressed just like that person. I call this *a hitchhiking spirit* that transfers from one person to the next. Sometimes you will see this when you keep company with someone and then start acting like them.

There are also *retaliating spirits*. Have you ever ministered to someone, and then every problem area in your life attacked all at once? Or maybe right before the Holy Spirit asked you to speak a word to someone, everything goes haywire? These are called retaliating Spirits. They are trying to stop your call, propose, and the anointing on you.

Some examples are your car breaking down or you get into an accident. You might also argue with a family member or coworker which whom you normally don't have arguments.

These demons attack because they're unhappy you are doing what God's called you to do. You can stop the hitchhiking and retaliating spirits, making them null and void by the power of the blood of Yeshua.

> ***Prayer:*** *Heavenly Father, I thank You for calling me for this time. Thank you for giving me a call and purpose to further Your kingdom and to glorify Your Holy Name. These demons want to scare me and make me think it's not worth doing Your will in these last days. I come against hitching and*

retaliating spirits and destroy their power over me.
I make them null and void. In Yeshua's, Amen

FIERY DARTS

"Above all, taking the shield of faith with which, you will be able to quench all the fiery darts of the wicked one." (Ephesians 6:16)

When I was young, there was a saying, "Sticks and stones may break my bones, but words can never hurt me." Words can hurt very badly, and words can be *fiery darts*. These hurtful words cause your heart to ache, and your mind grinds over them repeatedly.

Have you ever had someone say something to you that hurt?

One morning, I was hurt, not angry or unforgiving. My mind replayed what happened between the offending person and me—my heart felt heavy. I sat down and prayed, "Lord, I don't understand. I am not angry, I am hurt, and I can't stop obsessing about what has been said." The Lord said, "That's a fiery dart, quench the fire with the blood of Yeshua; pull the dart out and apply the living water from under my throne to wash out the cut, then apply my blood over the wound." As I did as instructed, the Lord lifted the heavy weight off of my heart. I repeated the same process to heal my mind. Instantly the thoughts stopped, and I had peace. I forgot what had upset me so much in the first place.

If you have a fiery dart and someone has wounded you with their words, pray this prayer.

> ***Prayer:*** *Father, I quench the fire of this fiery dart with the blood of Yeshua, and I remove the dart from my heart and mind; I send it to the abyss. I pray for the living water from under Your throne to cleanse the wound; I apply the blood of Yeshua that was shed for me at Calvary to the wound to bring complete healing. Thank You, Abba. In Yeshua's name, Amen.*

CHAPTER TWENTY-TWO
Prayer and Fasting

We are in the Kingdom of God; we are kingdom carriers, we are in His army, and we are in spiritual warfare.

"Is this not the fast that I have chosen: To lose the bonds of wickedness, to undo the heavy burdens, to let the oppressed go free, and that you break every yoke?" (Isaiah 58:6)

This scripture shows that God requires us to choose to *fast* as part of spiritual warfare. Fasting is repeatedly referred to throughout scripture as a sacrificial form of spiritual warfare that produces results available in no other way.

In 2 Chronicles 20:1-28, we learn of an event that occurred during the rule of Jehoshaphat. An army was coming against Jehoshaphat and the people of Judah. He was fearful yet sought the Lord and declared a fast in all the land. In addition to prayer and fasting, the people of Judah worshipped the Lord with praise and thanksgiving. God responded by telling all of Judah that the battle was not theirs but His, for He was with them. They entered the battle with praise and worship. The enemy nations destroyed one another, and no one escaped death. Jehoshaphat and his army took the spoils from the enemy and returned to Jerusalem joyfully, for the Lord made them victorious over their enemies. This account exemplifies how the power of prayer and fasting, mixed with praise, is a wonderful defense tool.

Another example we find is in Matthew 17. In this chapter, a man brought his epileptic son to the disciples for deliverance, but they could not cast out the demon. Yeshua rebuked the demon; the demon came out, and the boy was healed. The disciples asked why they could not cast it out, and Jesus replied, *"So, Jesus said to them, 'Because of your unbelief; for assuredly, I say to you, if you have faith as a mustard seed, you will say to this mountain, 'Move from here to there,' and it will move; and nothing will be impossible for you. However, this kind does not go out except by prayer and fasting."* (Matthew 17:20-21)

Yeshua noted the power of *prayer* and *fasting* in demonic deliverance by indicating, "this kind does not come out but by prayer and fasting." This step is vital to a deliverance ministry and is a powerful weapon against darkness.

Let's review another testimony of the power of fasting in the book of Esther. She was an orphan adopted by her cousin. It is easy to imagine that she struggled with abandonment issues, hurts, and pains of the heart. God had a calling and purpose for her life. God's favor for her shone through the King, as he loved her more than all the other women and made her queen. Outside the palace, the Jews were being served a terrible fate; Haman, the overseer of all the princes, issued an order to kill Jews, both young and old, and plunder their possessions. Upon learning of this fate, Esther called a fast.

> *"Go, gather all the Jews who are present in Shushan, and fast for me; neither eat nor drink for three days, night or day. My maids and I will fast likewise. And so, I will go to the King, which is against the law; and if I perish, I perish!" (Esther 4:16)*

The power of fasting is evident through the salvation of the Jewish people. The King was angered by Haman's plot to kill the Jews. Through a decree from the King, their lives were spared, and favor was granted to them.

Then we read their response to the news.

> *"The Jews had light and gladness, joy, and honor. And in every province and city, wherever the King's command and decree came, the Jews had joy and*

gladness, a feast, and a holiday. Then many of the people of the land became Jews because fear of the Jews fell upon them." (Esther 8:16-17)

Esther was called to help undo the heavy burdens and let the oppressed go free. God would break that yoke. Mordecai told Esther she had been placed in the King's house for such a time like this. And fasting was the weapon she used.

For the Hebrews, bondage and sentence of death were replaced with life and freedom through fasting. The above scriptures state, "Then many of the people become Jews."

I believe as we fast and pray, we, too, will defeat our enemy, and many people will come to know the Lord.

ONE EXAMPLE IN MY OWN LIFE WITH PRAYER AND FASTING

I learned about fasting when I was eighteen. I was a new Christian—having just received Yeshua as my Lord and Savior. My earthly father, who is now with the Lord, was an alcoholic. I loved my father. He was an incredible man in many ways. Even though he had a rugged exterior, he was unselfish, and he had a good heart. So, when I found the Lord, my dad was at the top of my list of people I hoped would receive Yeshua as Lord and Savior. If you knew him back then, that seemed to be an impossible request.

I decided to fast for my father and started praying all morning for my dad's salvation. Around five o'clock in the afternoon, the phone rang. My mother told me my father was having emergency surgery. He had blood clots in his lungs and heart. It was dire, and she wanted me to have a chance to speak to him before the operation. They did not know if he would make it through the surgery.

I had about 90 minutes to drive to the hospital. I was furious at God. I didn't understand His purpose and plan. I didn't know why He would have me pray for people only to see things worsen. But sometimes, things get worse before they get better.

My dad made it through the surgery. He started telling me about his hospital experience. He had died on that operating table and had left his body. He had an out-of-body experience. He met Yeshua and received the Lord when I was fasting and praying for him.

You may have someone in your family like this. You think they can't possibly change because they are in the world of drugs, alcohol, or perversion. Is your marriage suffering? Is your heart broken because you've been disappointed? Is there strife in your home— not unity or love? The oneness you were hoping for is not there. Do you need a breakthrough in your finances? Is there something that keeps you up at night, and you have done everything you can do, yet nothing is changing? Are you struggling with your walk with the Lord or even in private sin? Do you need a miracle in your life? You have a weapon that can produce miracles. Fasting can give you that spiritual breakthrough that you need and are seeking.

A *fast* is a time without food. The Church today is not used to denying their flesh, and Satan has caused many believers to experience a medical or physical condition that makes fasting food difficult. If you have physical conditions, I suggest protein drinks, juices, and broths–these can be helpful. Ask God to show you which fast He has chosen for your special need.

As we've seen above, many biblical fasts are gripped by crises and are an appeal to God for deliverance. Yeshua instructs us to fast. *"Moreover, when you fast, do not be like the hypocrites, with a sad countenance. For they disfigure their faces that they may appear to men to be fasting. Assuredly, I say to you, they have their reward. But you, when you fast, anoint your head and wash your face, so that you do not appear to men to be fasting, but to your Father who is in the secret place; and your Father who sees in secret will reward you openly."* (Matthew 6:16-18)

Fasting is a condition of the heart, with pure motives, where you seek the Lord and overturn the enemy's power through spiritual discipline.

Follow the steps on the following page.

- Set time aside to pray and find a quiet place. You must have time to talk to God and for Him to speak and minister to you.

- Ask your Heavenly Father to put a hedge around you and cover yourself with the blood of Yeshua.

Pray the following prayer:

Prayer: *Father, I humble myself before You, and I ask that You take me into your chosen fast to lose the bonds of wickedness, to undo the heavy burdens, to let the oppressed go free, and break every yoke and chain. Give me the enabling grace to fast In Yeshua's name, Amen.*

Closing Thoughts

"Then the seventy returned with joy, saying, "Lord, even the demons are subject to us in Your name."

And He said to them, "I saw Satan fall like lightning from heaven. Behold, I give you the authority to trample on serpents and scorpions, and over all the power of the enemy, and nothing shall by any means hurt you. Nevertheless, do not rejoice in this, that the spirits are subject to you, but rather rejoice because your names are written in heaven." (Luke 10:17-20)

"And they overcame him by the blood of the Lamb and by the word of their testimony, and they did not love their lives to the death." (Revelation 12:11)

MY PRAYER FOR YOU:

"May the Lord bless and keep you; may the Lord make His face shine upon you and be gracious to you. The Lord lifts up His countenance upon you and gives you peace."

This scripture is a blessing given by God to the people. It is taken from Numbers 6:24-16.

About The Author

Dr. Patricia Venegas is the Co-founder (with her husband, Rev Benjamin), Executive Director, and Senior Pastor of Without Spot or Wrinkle Ministries Intl. founded in 1998 in La Verne, California. In addition to the church in La Verne she has planted churches in Boerne, Texas., and Albuquerque, New Mexico.

She has a bachelor's in theology, a master's in religious studies with an emphasis on Christian Counseling, a Doctor of Divinity, and is a certified behavioral analyst. She specializes in Pastoral Counseling.

She walks in a global apostolic anointing to restore the Bride of Christ, the Church, to be glorious, without spot or wrinkle, to be ready for the second coming of our Lord and Savior,

Jesus/Yeshua. (Ephesians 5:26). Her anointing equips the believer in God's army with the tools necessary to fight spiritual battles using boldness and unwavering faith, using the Word of God as a spiritual sword. (Ephesians 6:17)

She served as a Chaplain with Covina California, Police Department, for 21 years, from 1999-2020.

She is an artist of fine art and the author of two books, *The Bride of Christ Without Spot or Wrinkle* and *Spiritual Boot Camp, Basic Training For Spiritual Warfare*, and many conference syllabi; she is the keynote speaker.

She is a sought-after speaker and travels the nations ministering to the brokenhearted with a heart of love and compassion.

Website: wosow.org.
Facebook: wosow Intl
YouTube channel: Dr. Patricia Venegas
and WOSOW Intl.
Office Phone: 909-593-2607

www.ingramcontent.com/pod-product-compliance
Lightning Source LLC
Chambersburg PA
CBHW070537090426
42735CB00013B/3004